Anaïs Nin

Twayne's United States Authors Series

Warren French, Editor
Indiana University, Indianapolis

TUSAS 460

ANAÏS NIN
(1903–1977)
Photograph courtesy of
Museum of Fine Arts, Boston
A. Shuman Collection

Anaïs Nin

By Nancy Scholar

Twayne Publishers • *Boston*

Anaïs Nin

Nancy Scholar

Copyright © 1984 by G. K. Hall & Company
All Rights Reserved
Published by Twayne Publishers
A Division of G. K. Hall & Company
70 Lincoln Street
Boston, Massachusetts 02111

Book Production by Marne B. Sultz

Book Design by Barbara Anderson

Printed on permanent/durable acid-free
paper and bound in the United States of
America.

**Library of Congress Cataloging in
Publication Data**

Scholar, Nancy, 1943–
Anaïs Nin.

(Twayne's United States authors series ;
TUSAS 460)
Bibliography: p. 141
Includes index.
1. Nin, Anaïs, 1903–1977—
Criticism and interpretation.
I. Title. II. Series.
PS3527.I865Z913   1984 818'.5209
83-26583
ISBN 0-8057-7400-9

For Don

Contents

About the Author

Nancy Scholar was born in 1943 in Clifton, New Jersey. She earned her undergraduate degree from Douglass College and her Ph.D. from Brown University. She has taught at several colleges including University of Illinois, Chicago Circle, Illinois Institute of Technology, Tufts University, and University of New Orleans. Her articles on women writers and film and literature have appeared in journals such as *Literature/Film Quarterly, Michigan Quarterly Review,* and a collection entitled *Sexual Strategems, The World of Women in Film.* She has taught a wide range of courses such as Dual Perspectives on Women in Modern Fiction, Expressionism and Surrealism in Art and Literature, and Images of the South in Film and Literature. Currently she lives in New Orleans.

Preface

Anaïs Nin, who has been called the "best-known diarist since Samuel Pepys,"[1] died in 1977, leaving behind a life-long diary of immense proportions. Approximately 3300 pages out of about 15,000 original diary pages are now in print, with more to come.[2] This monumental work has variously been described as a *"cathedral* of her *ego,"* the "only sustained meditation on art that exists in the literature of the U.S.," and "the most complete documentation of one woman's subjective life ever made available to the general public."[3] Nin has been treated to a good deal of abuse as well as to cult worship ad nauseam, but rarely to serious study. The predominant tone in the book-length studies published to date has been "appreciative," but hardly critical.[4]

"Of all the forms of literature," Joyce Carol Oates has commented, "the diary is perhaps the most seductive for both reader and writer." We are "hypnotized by the conviction that *this is real:* therefore it must have value."[5] This is precisely what has happened with innumerable readers and critics of Nin's Diary. They are charmed, beguiled, distracted from aesthetic considerations with the false impression that it is "life" not "art" they are witnessing. It is this conviction of authenticity that I examine in this book, along with the art of seduction at which Nin excelled, as her popular erotica testifies. I also study the many masks Nin wears in her writing as a method of allurement and protection. Through the images of the mirror and window which proliferate in the text, I consider the extent of Nin's subjectivity, the quality of her perceptions of the outer world. I try to focus on those aspects of her Diary and fiction—another variation on her self-portrait—that are most worthy of consideration, richest in what they have to teach. My conviction that the Diary is an important, if flawed work, while the fiction is secondary in value, determines my emphasis in the limited space available on Nin's most significant autobiographical achievement. Throughout the book, I aim to be sympathetic to Nin's struggles as a woman artist, while not being blind to her shortcomings as a writer. By placing her work in the context of an autobiographical as well as a female literary tradition,[6] I hope to show both its representativeness as well as its unique attributes.

I wish to thank my husband, Don, for his loving support and willingness to read innumerable drafts, my dear friend Jeanne Anderegg, who read it all and offered helpful feedback, as did Jean Thompson, Richard Weaver, and Russell Young. I also am most grateful for the encouragement and assistance of my editor, Warren French, as well as the Boston editor, John LaBine. In addition, I wish to thank Keith Waldrop for encouraging me years ago in my writing on Nin, and Sharon Spencer for suggesting this particular project.

Excerpts from *The Diary of Anaïs Nin,* volumes I, II, III, IV, V, VI, VII; *Linotte, The Early Diary of Anaïs Nin,* volume I; and *The Early Diary of Anaïs Nin,* volume II are reprinted by permission of Harcourt Brace Jovanovich, Inc., © 1966, 1967, 1971, 1974, 1976 by Anaïs Nin; © 1978, 1980, 1982 by Rupert Pole as trustee under the Last Will and Testament of Anaïs Nin.

Excerpts from *House of Incest* by Anaïs Nin, © 1958 by Anaïs Nin; from *Under A Glass Bell* by Anaïs Nin, copyright 1948 by Anaïs Nin, © renewed 1976 by Anaïs Nin; from *Winter of Artifice* by Anaïs Nin, copyright 1945, 1946, 1948 by Anaïs Nin, © renewed 1973 by Anaïs Nin; from *Ladders to Fire* by Anaïs Nin, copyright 1946, © 1959, 1963 by Anaïs Nin; © renewed © 1974 by Anaïs Nin; from *Children of the Albatross* by Anaïs Nin, Copyright 1947, © 1959 by Anaïs Nin, © renewed 1975 by Anaïs Nin; from *The Four-Chambered Heart* by Anaïs Nin, copyright 1950, © 1959 by Anaïs Nin, © renewed 1978 by the Anaïs Nin Trust; from *A Spy in the House of Love* by Anaïs Nin, copyright 1954, © 1959 by Anaïs Nin, © renewed 1982 by the Anaïs Nin Trust; from *Seduction of the Minotaur* by Anaïs Nin, © 1961 by Anaïs Nin; from *Collages* by Anaïs Nin, © 1964 by Anaïs Nin. All rights reserved. Reprinted by permission of the Author's Representative, Gunther Stuhlmann.

Nancy Scholar

Chronology

1903	Anaïs Nin born 21 February in Neuilly, France.
1914	Left Barcelona for New York with mother and two brothers. Began life-long diary.
1919	Dropped out of Wadleigh High School in New York. Family moved from 158 West 75th Street to Richmond Hill.
1922	Worked as artist's model. Taken to Cuba by wealthy aunt.
1923	Married Hugh P. Guiler in Cuba.
1931	Met Henry and June Miller.
1932	*D. H. Lawrence. An Unprofessional Study.* Psychoanalysis with Dr. René Allendy.
1933	Reunited with father. Began psychoanalysis with Dr. Otto Rank. Met Antonin Artaud.
1934	Delivered a stillborn child. Joined Rank in New York, practiced lay analysis with him.
1935	Returned to Louveciennes, her home outside Paris.
1936	*The House of Incest.* Purchased houseboat.
1937	Met Lawrence Durrell.
1939–1940	*The Winter of Artifice.* Returned to New York. Met Robert Duncan, Luise Rainer, Edgar and Louise Vàrese, Kenneth Patchen, Dorothy Norman. Began writing erotica for a collector.
1942	Set up her own printing press, Gemor Press. Printed revised *Winter of Artifice.* Analysis with Martha Jaeger.
1944	Printed *Under a Glass Bell.* Met Edmund Wilson.
1945	Printed *This Hunger.* Met Gore Vidal.
1946	*Ladders to Fire.* Acted in Maya Deren film.
1947	*Children of the Albatross.* Cross-country tour with friend. Met Lloyd Wright, Janko Varda, James Herlihy.

1948   Acted in Kenneth Anger film. Began travel between New
       York, California, Mexico.

1949   Father died in Cuba.

1950   *The Four-Chambered Heart.*

1951   Began analysis with Dr. Inge Bogner. Acted in Ian Hugo's
       film, *Bells of Atlantis.*

1953   Met Renate Druks.

1954   Mother died in California. *A Spy in the House of Love.*

1958   *Solar Barque.*

1959   *Cities of the Interior* first published. Met Marguerite Young.

1961   Bought house in mountains above Los Angeles. Alan Swal-
       low took over publication and distribution of her fiction.

1964   *Collages.*

1966   *The Diary of Anaïs Nin: 1931–1934.* Began to lecture
       widely.

1967   *The Diary of Anaïs Nin: 1934–1939.*

1968   *The Novel of the Future.*

1969   *The Diary of Anaïs Nin: 1939–1944.*

1971   *The Diary of Anaïs Nin: 1944–1947.* Awarded France's Prix
       Sevigne.

1973   Received honorary Doctorate of Art from Philadelphia
       College of Art.

1974   Elected to National Institute of Arts and Letters. Received
       honorary doctorate from Dartmouth College. *The Diary of
       Anaïs Nin: 1947–1955.*

1976   *The Diary of Anaïs Nin: 1955–1966. In Favor of the Sensitive
       Man and Other Essays.*

1977   Nin died of cancer in Los Angeles, 14 January. *Delta of
       Venus. Erotica.*

1978   *Linotte. The Early Diary of Anaïs Nin: 1914–1920.*

1979   *Little Birds. Erotica.*

1980   *The Diary of Anaïs Nin: 1966–1974.*

1982   *The Early Diary of Anaïs Nin: 1920–1923.*

Chapter One
Her Life as Art
Origins

Attempting to set out the "facts" of Anaïs Nin's life is a hazardous enterprise. Nin made an art out of her life, and made her life the subject of her art. Distinguishing between the two is difficult if not impossible. Nin worked to dissolve the boundary between dream and reality, to erase the certainties of existence which she regarded as burdensome. Her lifetime occupation was the re-creation of her life in her Diary, begun at eleven years old, concluded only with her death at seventy-three. "I was telling myself the story of a life," she explained in a speech in 1973, "and this transmutes into an adventure the things which can shatter you" (VII, 266).[1] In turning to Nin's Diary for our version of Nin's life (no other options are currently available), we must keep in mind that our source is only a "story of a life," just as the "Nin" to whom we refer throughout this book is only the main character in that story. "Anaïs Nin" takes shape and form through her Diary, ultimately unknown to herself and her readers outside its pages. "Yes, my life flows into ink!" she declared exultantly in her Diary at eighteen, relishing even then her transformation in the Diary which brings her into being, makes her known to herself and the world. On the vast tapestry which is Nin's life-book, she embroiders the legend of her existence, adding colors and shading as she proceeds.

Nin began composing the story of her life on the journey from Barcelona to New York when she was eleven years old, but her actual birth date was 21 February 1903 in Neuilly, France. Rosa Culmel, her mother, was a singer of French-Danish descent and Joaquin Nin, her father, was a concert pianist of Spanish origin, although both were born in Cuba. According to Nin, her maternal great grandfather left France during the Revolution for Haiti, New Orleans, and finally Cuba where he built the first railroad. Her maternal grandmother was a "New Orleans beauty" who deserted husband and children for a lover, perhaps a character similar to Kate Chopin's daring heroine in *The Awakening*. Although Nin refers to her father's descent from Spanish aristocracy, his exact origins are unknown. According to the Diary, Joaquin Nin spent his time concertizing and womanizing around Europe, returning home sporadically to engage in verbal combat with Nin's mother, to criticize and sometimes abuse Anaïs and her two brothers, Thorvald and Joaquin. He also brought with him a glamorous world of high culture, exposing Nin to books, music, and musicians, whetting her appetite for the artistic life. After living, among other places, in Berlin, Brussels, and in a ruined castle in Arcachon, the scene of the father's final desertion, the mother and children moved to Barcelona from whence they departed for New York in 1914.

Nin's Diary began as her "ship," a communicating vessel in her imagination between herself and her father. Its purpose originally was to persuade her father to join them, and to convince him of her own uniqueness, in doubt as a result of his desertion which she naturally interpreted as related to her own deficiencies. This childhood Diary grew in importance as the pages accumulated, becoming a "magic mirror," a method of self-transformation, and a "shell" or "nest," protecting a fragile ego still mending from early wounds. Her father's significance was magnified as the distance between them grew. He turned into a "mystery, a vision, a dream" to the adolescent girl, a "dearly beloved shadow" intertwined in her mind with her journal, also designated her "shadow." He came to embody the ideal Artist she aspired to be, and his writings on the sanctified role of the artist, in the late nineteenth-century tradition, may well have fed her fantasy of the artist's grandiose role.[2] But her longing to emulate this distant god was disturbed by persistent reminders, primarily from her mother, of his darker qualities inimical to her notion of femininity—selfishness, sexual adventurousness, above all. The fact that he failed to appear after the young dreamer attempted to will his presence on more than one occasion further diminished her enthusiasm for this noble ideal.

Nin also wished to emulate her mother during adolescence, referring to her in the second early Diary published since Nin's death as "the woman nearest perfection in the world." Her early journals are full of praise for this self-abnegating and courageous woman who raised three children on her own in New York. Rosa Culmel worked diligently to improve the status of her family, setting up a business of shopping for her wealthy Cuban relatives on consignment, doing well enough to move her family from the city to a large house in Richmond Hill. She assigned her daughter the role of mother's assistant, giving Nin bookkeeping and housekeeping chores regularly, but apparently Anaïs was too dreamy to succeed at her tasks. As her mother's "little philosopher," however, she was a source of pride. This was not based on excellence in schooling, seemingly a matter of little interest to Nin, who dropped out of Wadleigh High School in 1919, picking up a few courses at Columbia University a bit later, but not staying there long. Instead, she distinguished herself by her incessant writing in her journal, for which she had great ambitions from an early age.

By the conclusion of the second early Diary, it is apparent this "perfect" mother was also a bit of a domestic tyrant, determined to maintain control over her daughter's life, wishing them to live together forever, to instill in Nin's mind the notion of her helplessness without her mother's assistance. Perhaps because of this, she virtually disappears from Nin's published Diary until her death in 1954, at which point, Nin reviews her deeply ambivalent attitude toward her mother and fills in the portrait only half-sketched in the early Diaries. It now appears that Rosa demanded at least as much as she gave. Rather than playing the supportive role to the burgeoning artist, Nin implies that Rosa mocked the ambitions of her daughter (at least occasionally) and even competed with her, singing for the young men who came courting Anaïs at sixteen. Only the ideal Rosa, however, appears in the early Diary, no doubt the product as much of Nin's needs at the time, as of her mother's closeness to her daughter and her text. Retrospectively, Nin informs us her mother symbolized the sort of woman she wished not to be, the woman "who capitulated to wifehood and motherhood." Nin was determined from a young age, she tells us later, "not to be like her but like the women who had enchanted and seduced" her father, the "mistresses who lured him away" from her (V, 182). Yet her Diary reveals both images of woman—the maternal as well as the seductive.

The Early Diaries

In the two early volumes published since Nin's death, covering the years 1914–1923, we can observe the shaping of the artist through a revealing and charming text. At thirteen years old, the immense ambition of the young writer is already apparent, as is her chafing at the restrictions of her sex. She feels frustrated that she can't "put on a man's skin" and fight for France, she says in *Linotte,* the earliest volume, but she decides her bayonet will be her pen. In mock humility she declares: "I am nothing but dust, made to be walked on." And then goes on, "Only I am a little bit ambitious, and I who am dust, I want to spread myself on a lot of paper, turn into lots of sentences, lots of words so that I won't be walked on" (L, 145). If the pen is to be the instrument of her freedom, the Diary is already designated the vehicle for her fame which she so clearly craves. At fourteen, she confides that her "vocation is to seek applause," and by seventeen she is referring to her "well-known little Diary." "I will make the *world listen to unseen and delicate music*" (E, 139), she predicts the following year.

Her Diary begins to take on a life of its own, even to supersede reality for the diarist. "To melt into one Book—my Life!" she exults at seventeen, revealing the extent to which her "Book" has already become indistinguishable from her "Life." "Did you know," she remarks, "that whatever I do or think I am always forming into words so that I may be able to tell you about it as perfectly as possible?" (E, 51). A simple existence is denied her; she must always be reshaping her life to suit the more demanding requirements of art. Making her life into an endless story, she perhaps inadvertently condemns herself to the role of spectator of her own existence. "I feel as if all the adventures which succeed one another were unfolding themselves like a play in a theatre—and I, miles and miles away, watching" (E, 77–78), she comments wistfully. Her book compels her to be an "Outsider," as she calls herself at a young age, but there are consolations in her solitary universe, her "shell life." Her distance from the drama of (her) life gives her a comforting sense of detachment from the painful side of existence. Also her "little lighthouse, constant and inspiring," soothes and controls her, as she puts it. "For after writing, I feel *reasonable,* and before acting, I pause to ask myself: Will I be ashamed to write this in my Diary?" (E, 158).

When Nin discovers Marie Bashkirtseff's *Journal* at eighteen, she finds a confirmation of her life-work perhaps unavailable elsewhere. "There are things she says," Nin remarks about Bashkirtseff's *Journal,* "that are reflected word for word here in my own diary. It's enough to make me think I am mad and that I copied them—or else that Marie's soul has been reincarnated in me!" (E, 291). The similarities between the two are remarkable, including an early craving for fame and admiration, along with a penchant for mirror-gazing. But Marie's blatant self-satisfaction with her reflection is unthinkable to the young Anaïs, more ambivalent about her self-image and possibly more aware of her audience at this age. "I looked all of a sudden so beautiful, after I had taken my bath this evening," Marie records, "that I spent fully twenty minutes admiring myself in the glass."³ Despite Nin's distaste for such complacency, Bashkirtseff's *Journal* makes a deep impression, bolstering her sense of the validity of her life-task, enabling her to see the prospect for charming one's audience through candor. "She has a thousand faults," Nin observes quite shrewdly, "and yet she captivates by her intelligence and originality. I have never been so divided between like and dislike, admiration and disapproval. . ." (E, 290). Perhaps through her experience of being captivated by Marie Bashkirtseff's *Journal,* the young Anaïs realizes for the first time just how seductive a diary could be, as well as how subject to disapproval.

Her growing conviction that writing in her life-book is a sacred mission intensifies in this second early Diary, especially after Nin discovers Emerson's essays—"Self-Reliance," in particular. This "giver-of-freedom" entreats her to *"speak,"* drawing her with even "greater strength" to her pen. When self-doubts creep in, she chants Emerson's words for relief: "Self-trust is the essence of heroism." He reassures her that her innermost thoughts can have profound significance, can link her with the "Outside World" she usually views from a distance. His creed of life as a continual process of growth also encourages her to perceive her own life-story in these terms. Emerson's disdain for conformity, too, must have been a helpful counterweight to her mother's desire to see her daughter turn into the perfect Woman.

All experience is grist for the mill of Nin's life-book. Activities are considered for their story potential, new friends are a "fresh collection of characters." Private emotion becomes public act, and feeling suspect as a result. She records yearning for Prince Charming, her Knight of Knights, long before he exists, so much so that when he finally appears, his reality is questioned as much by Nin as by her readers. This "Magician of Happiness," as she calls him, is Hugh (Hugo) Guiler, banker and financier, later known as Ian Hugo, engraver and filmmaker. The fact that this man, whom Nin married in 1923 in Cuba, is absent from the Diary as she published it, does not increase his substantiality. But he is very much the subject of the second early Diary published since Nin's death. Hugo helps bring Nin out of the "oyster shell" of her life-book. "I have ceased to be the Outsider and Onlooker," Nin declares after realizing their love is mutual. "I am *part* of what I wish to describe. I live! I live! I live!" (419). The love she imagined for so long finally has a tangible reality, but she worries at times that it is an imaginative construction. She also grows concerned about the compatibility of her roles as woman and artist. "If the writer in me requires a life that will supply food to the imagination," she wonders at nineteen, "will it survive between four walls and in caring for home and husband?" (E, 449). Determined to submerge neither woman nor writer, she nevertheless fears marriage will force a choice upon her.

As if in defiance of this possibility, she embarks on an adventure immediately after her engagement, traveling to Woodstock, New York, to model for the artists, as she had done in the city for months before. This jaunt fills her with a *"sense of power"* as an artist and an exhilarating feeling of "Freedom unbounded." The voluminous writing she is able to do during this interlude confirms the artist in her, while modeling reinforces the woman. Dressed in her Watteau costume "which suited her to perfection," Nin recalls in Diary II, she was the star model of the Model's Club for a time, literally the art object for a miriad artists and magazine readers that she was in her own life-book. Her need as a young woman to be admired, thought beautiful, is fulfilled and perhaps dangerously inten-sified by her role as artist's model, threatening to submerge the artist within. Her stint as a Spanish dancer may have had the same effect, although this chapter in Nin's life has yet to be revealed (in the two volumes to be published).

Major Influences

The opening of Diary I makes clear, however, that the writer in Nin is in no real danger of submergence. In fact, one of the distinguishing features of this legendary personality is her remarkable pertinacity in fulfilling childhood literary ambitions, regardless of obstacles such as traditional female roles. When Diary I opens in 1931, Nin is certainly "between four walls" as she feared, confined to the "beautiful prison" of her antique house in Louveciennes, a Paris suburb, but she has already completed a book on D. H. Lawrence about to be published. She hopes this book will make a bridge with the world, which indeed it does, leading to her intimacy with Henry Miller, another Lawrence enthusiast, and to a wider audience in later years.

This "unprofessional study" of Lawrence, as Nin called it, was a pathbreaking book (1932), written at a time when Lawrence was under-valued, regarded by many as a poetic pornographer at best. Nin takes up his defense and does a fine job, earning Harry T. Moore's praise that it is "one of the most valuable books on Lawrence."[4] Lawrence was clearly another liberating force for Nin, much as Emerson had been. His dynamic view of life and personality as process had a similar appeal, along with his role as prophet of *"Livingness."* She praises his novels and poems as *"pure passionate experiences,"* while admiring his "mystical attitude" to the flesh. The emotional intensity and acuity of his vision make a great impression, as they are evident in the best of Nin's writing.

Most important is Lawrence's recognition of the "dark gods" within, his effort "to make conscious and articulate the silent subconscious communications between human beings" (16). This he does in a manner Nin praises as subtle and penetrating, particularly in his comprehension of the inner workings of woman. She regards his treatment of women as a whole as "extremely sympathetic," especially his understanding of how women had effaced their real selves "in order to satisfy man-made images. Men had the images, they conceived the patterns—women carried them out to please the men" (49). Perhaps through Lawrence, Nin awakens to the necessity for formulating her own patterns, becoming her own "artist-builder." But Lawrence also suggests that in doing so, she will threaten her femininity, thus sowing the seeds of Nin's self-doubts as a woman artist a bit deeper. Lawrence's effect on Nin's writing was also negative in some respects, encouraging her penchant for flat statement rather than dramatization, for a "repetitious and a solemn hieratic tone."[5]

Henry Miller's effect on Nin was similarly mixed, although largely positive on her as a writer. Both Nin and Miller produced some of their best writing—what was to become the first two Diaries, *House of Incest* on Nin's part, *Tropic of Cancer, Black Spring* on Miller's—during the years of their intimacy in Paris in the thirties. When they first met in 1931, Miller had manuscripts but no published book, and Nin had completed her Lawrence study, but had published no other writing. They each offered the other the support and encouragement as writers neither had previously enjoyed. This mutual support was probably more important than any influence either had on the other's work. Nin believed in Miller's literary genius, and this belief helped spawn the best of his works. Miller had the highest praise for Nin's journals, writing in *Criterion* in 1937 that her Diary would take its place "beside the revelations of St. Augustine, Petronius, Abélard, Rousseau, Proust and others."[6]

By the summer of 1932, Nin was supporting Miller, and by the end of 1933, he wanted to marry her, although she continued to derive emotional and financial support from her husband, Hugo.[7] The situation was complicated further by Miller's continued obsession with his estranged wife, June, who also became the object of Nin's obsessional interest, as she records in the first Diary. Miller also had a penchant for womanizing, for the low life, abundantly illustrated in his autobiographical fiction. Add to this Miller's need to be worshiped, no doubt in conflict with Nin's need for the same, and you have a problematic, though stimulating union. Nin was most inspired by Miller when he was uncertain of his capacities; once he became successful, with the publication of *Tropic of Cancer* (published through money Nin raised), there was trouble in paradise. Nonetheless, Nin continued to support Miller, maintaining him in his Villa Seurat studio throughout the thirties, helping later with periodic checks.

Villa Seurat became a meeting place for artists, including Lawrence Durrell who played the role of literary son to the parents, Miller and Nin. The three of them collaborated on publishing ventures, including a special Christmas issue of the magazine *The Booster* called "Air-Conditioned Womb Number," in which each played on the motif of the "womb," a favorite theme during this time. In 1939 Durrell put up the funds for three publications through Obelisk Press: Nin's *Winter of Artifice,* Miller's *Max and the White Phagocytes,* and Durrell's *Black Book.* According to Diary II, the three engaged in stimulating discussions about gender and creativity, autobiographical art, which challenged Nin to define more clearly her task in her life-book. Nin's second Diary is at its richest when she records her views on "woman's art" worked out in discussions with Miller and Durrell.

In addition, both Nin and Miller helped each other with the craft of writing. "We have much influence over each other's work," Nin comments in Diary I, "I on the artistry and insight, on the going beyond realism, he on the matter, substance, and vitality of mine. I have given him depth, and he gives me concreteness" (166). They both, in fact, influenced each other's "artistry," with Nin helping Miller sift through the masses of material he was pouring forth during the early thirties, and he carefully editing the materials she was producing. "Elaborate!" Miller declares after reading her "House" manuscript. "That is the only way out of these watertight abstractions of yours. Break through them, divest them of their mystery and allow them to flow" (198). Not only was Miller beneficial for Nin in his advocacy of less abstraction, more "flow" in her style, but also in his interpretation of her Diary which remains one of the most insightful.[8]

"Flow" is the key word in Miller's influence on Nin, as it is in Marcel Proust's. Repeatedly, Nin praises the quality of "flow and infinite continuum" in Proust's *Remembrance of Things Past* which she admired perhaps above all other works.[9] This continuous novel constructed out of Proust's memories recaptured was a perennial source of inspiration to Nin in her own task of reconstruction. If Proust could create such a monumental work without leaving his cork-lined study, then there was hope for Nin in her own subjective enterprise. Proust also confirmed Nin's belief in the unreality of the outer world, and the far deeper reality of the inner—an attitude common to the symbolists with whom Nin shared many attitudes.[10] She relished the mystery and indefiniteness of Proust's *Remembrance,* and the fact that his characters were only half-drawn, filled in over time, as are hers in the Diary. She notes that he "never fixed a date upon anything," thereby exonerating her own indifference to chronology. He is one of her three "gods of the deep," along with Lawrence and Dostoevsky, writers whose depths she never completely sounds.

Psychoanalysis

At least from 1932, when Nin began psychoanalysis with Dr. René Allendy, until her death in 1977, she maintained her adherence to the "modern religion" of psychoanalysis, believing it to be the "key to all other experiences," the "only way for us to achieve wholeness." Psychoanalysis is a major force in her life-work, the inspiration for some of her best writing in the Diary, for many of her most penetrating revelations. Yet her faith is subject to doubts. She fluctuates between a determination to enter the "labyrinth of analysis," to alter the damaging patterns of the past, and a desire to succumb to the rhythms of existence, untroubled by dissection. "Introspection is a devouring monster," she exclaims after analysis with Dr. Otto Rank, as she does sporadically throughout the Diary.

Nin's first record in the Diary of sessions with an analyst (Dr. Allendy) contribute greatly to the charm and sense of disarming candor of volume one. Allendy is portrayed at first as a magician, working his spell from his dark salon opening on a greenhouse. Before long, he has Nin discussing the complete artificiality of her personality, as if "enveloped in a mist, veiled." Her need to charm and seduce is fully revealed, although her wish to "surpass men" is vehemently denied by an indignant Nin: "I protected and sacrificed much for my brother's musical career, made it possible. I am now helping Henry and giving him all I can, to do his own work. I gave Henry my typewriter. There I think you are very wrong" (82). Accusations such as this, as well as Allendy's belief in "interior fatality," the ineluctable recurrence of patterns in human behavior due to unconscious impulses (reversible only with lengthy analysis) also discourages Nin from further effort. Rather than continue this excruciating exploration of her neurosis, Nin shifts her attention to seduction of the analyst. This is accomplished with seeming ease and dramatically displayed in a session in which she reverses roles with Allendy, getting him to sit in her chair, play analysand to her. She also manages a similar feat with her second analyst, Rank, who plays a more significant role in Nin's life-legend.

Even before Nin began analysis with Rank in 1933, she was interested in him because of his study of art and neurosis, *Art and Artist,* published in 1932. His elevation of the artist's role and approval of the artist's impulse to glorify him/herself was music to Nin's ears: "The precondition, then, of the creative personality is not only acceptance, but its actual glorification of itself" (I, 200). Nin's penchant for legendizing, idealizing herself, is now heralded as a manifestation of her creative personality. In contrast to Allendy, Rank delights in the mythology she has created around herself, helping her to elaborate further with his extensive socio-cultural perspective. Her obsessive love for her father is a variation of the age-old legend of father-daughter separation and reunion after twenty years. Her love for June Miller is not lesbianism, but another manifestation of the double theme, one of Rank's favorites, along with the nineteenth-century romantics he favors.

After Nin follows Rank to New York to assist him in his work and act as analyst herself, she depicts him as pouncing on each trivial event of her day, raising "this fragment to a brilliant, complete, dazzling legend." "I felt like an actress," she goes on, "who had not known how moving her voice and gestures had been, their tremendous repercussion, but also like a creator preparing in some dim laboratory a life like a legend, and now reading the legend itself from an enormous book. And this was certainly a part of the legend, Rank bowing over each incident, explaining, marveling at this miracle. . . ." (II, 39). The legend was of course well under way before Nin met Rank, but the "gift" he gave her "was that of being understood, justified, absolved."

Nin eventually reacts against analysis with Rank, partly because, according to Nin, he demanded too much of her, asking her to devote her life to translating his magnum opus on the incest theme. After attending a meeting of psychoanalysts, Nin realizes she does not belong in this world, where she will always feel like a "fraud," but in the artist's world. "The key word was the sea," she explains. "It was this oceanic life which was being put in bottles and labeled. Underneath my feet, moving restlessly beneath the very floor of the hotel, was the sea, and my nature which would never amalgamate with analysis in any permanent marriage" (II, 41). In addition, although Rank was immensely encouraging to Nin as an artist, assuring her that her Diary was valuable as a document of a woman's point of view, he was capable of saying, "When the neurotic woman gets cured, she becomes a woman. When the neurotic man gets cured, he becomes an artist" (I, 291). Rank also fought Nin's diary-writing habit, calling it her "last defense against analysis." Nin reached the moment with Rank when she "saw too much, unveiled too much, the psychological terminus."

Nonetheless, Nin is back in analysis in Diary III, this time with Martha Jaeger, a Jungian analyst who offers her a female viewpoint. Her third journal comes alive after a torpid period as Nin jots down in shorthand fashion the insights resulting from analysis:

I have a horror of the masculine "career" woman. To create seemed to me such an assertion of the strongest part of me that I would no longer be able to give all those I love the feeling of their being stronger, and they would love me less. . . . I would be abandoned by all those I loved. Men fear woman's strength. I have been deeply aware of men's weakness, the need to guard them from my strength. I have made myself less powerful, have concealed my powers . . . I have crippled myself.
Dreams of Chinese women with bound feet.
I have bound myself spiritually . . . I see strongly creative women crush their men . . . I have feared all aggressiveness, all attacks, all destruction. Above all, self-assertion. (259–60)

Jaeger enables Nin to see the connection between her creative blocks and traditional feminine imperatives, such as the guilt for creating, the stigma against assertiveness. Although this represents more a moment of insight than a turning point in Nin's life, given her continued propensity for maternal self-sacrifice, it is nevertheless persuasive. Eventually, however, Jaeger is stripped of her powers in relation to Nin, much as Allendy and Rank were earlier. Nin develops a personal relationship with Jaeger which means the inevitable demise of their analytic relationship. Not only does Nin become aware of Jaeger's personal failings, but Jaeger expresses reservations about Nin's writing. Jaeger's role in this drama essentially ceases thereafter.

Similarly, Nin has a crisis in confidence with her last analyst, Dr. Inge Bogner, when she too raises questions about Nin's work. But Nin does not give up on Bogner, and in recording their debate on this issue, Nin enriches her text. In Diary V and again in VI, Nin refers to a discussion about the extent of her subjectivity. Nin admits she became very disturbed at the implication that she demonstrated extreme subjectivity in her writing. Bogner's criticism, painful as it evidently was to Nin, seems to have struck a respondent chord. Nin's sacrosanct notion about the quality of her perceptions apparently crumbled at her feet; she was no longer certain that her Diary was a perfect mirror for others. "We are like sculptors, constantly carving out of others the image we long for, need, love or desire," Nin observes in Diary VI, "often against reality, against their benefit, and always, in the end, a disappointment because it does not fit them" (17–18). Through analysis with Bogner and others, Nin is able to come out from behind the ideal mask she wears too often in the Diary, and to express human fallibilities that make her as a character and her Diary more persuasive.

The Voyage

After Nin returns to Paris from her interlude in New York with Rank, she enters a new phase as an artist, epitomized by her purchase of a houseboat, *La Belle Aurore.* The decision to acquire the houseboat immediately follows a discussion with Henry Miller in which Nin resolves to make more of her Diary, her "malady." The houseboat is evidence of Nin's determination to make her life more worthy of her art, as well to turn dream into reality. The dream comes after Nin visited the home formerly owned by Guy de Maupassant. Fascinated by a deserted fishing boat lodged in the garden, Nin dreams about it and writes an early short story, "Waste of Timelessness."[11]

In this charming little tale, Nin narrates the story of a young woman bored with the "usual houseparty" and the "usual husband" who finds an ancient fishing boat "waiting in the dark garden, at the end of the very narrow path." Into this womblike atmosphere, the disaffected young woman gladly surrenders herself for the night, wishing before repose that there were some way to begin life anew, having made a bad beginning. Her wish is answered in a dream of setting sail on a river without end for a twenty-year journey. "What *are* you headed for?" her husband shouts at her from the shore. "Something big," she replies, as she glides away. She attempts to pay a visit to the "great writer," Roussel, but he is surrounded by "ecstatic worshippers." After passing him again, she realizes she has "travelled in a circle." Roussel calls out to her that she has "run away from life," an accusation Nin is to hear from many men. Her journey ends at this point with the demure apology, "I have been wasting a lot of time," but the title indicates otherwise. It is *timelessness* Nin is after, and the circular journey without end she imagines—a perfect description of what is to become Nin's Diary—is her pathway to that goal.

Throughout the Diary, Nin associates her life-work with the boat and journey motifs, as well as the womb, cave, and labyrinth, all related images in Nin's writing. Her houseboat is perfectly suited to her book, since it is a ship, but a domestic, interior vessel, like her journal. It is particularly appropriate for the second Diary in which Nin is most interested in defining her work as a woman. Her houseboat also marks the distance Nin has traveled from her analytic experience with Rank in New York. She is now in reaction against "dissection," happily adrift on the Seine.

Her houseboat also provides the setting for rendezvous with Gonzalo, romantic lead in Diary II, who offers Nin Peruvian legends, proximity to revolutionary activities, and passionate devotion. To compensate for forbidden pleasures apparently enjoyed on board this craft, Nin plays the part of domestic saint to perfection in volume two, tending to the frequently sotted Gonzalo and his destructive, psychopathic wife Helba with undeniable zeal. In his role as Spanish republican, Gonzalo challenges Nin's antipolitical stance, briefly engages her in the politics of the time, but ultimately only confirms her own convictions in the personal basis for all political acts. With increasing defensiveness, Nin justifies her belief in the artist's prerogative to create an individually perfect world, despite the surrounding madness. Her houseboat becomes the symbol of this choice, her "Noah's Ark," haven and retreat for the artist from the disintegrating society at large.

At the end of Diary II, however, Nin is forced to retire her vessel as World War II impinges on her Ark. She and her husband return full circle to New York, but things are never quite the same. The romance of the Paris years has ended, and with it, the spirit of the best of the Diaries. Miller is in Greece and Nin drydocked in what she regards as the sordid, insensitive New World. Her voyage towards "something big" is impeded time and again by unfriendly book reviewers and unwilling publishers. She becomes increasingly obsessed with this wall of indifference to her work, finding a temporary solution when she sets up her own printing press in Greenwich Village in 1942. On her Gemor Press with the assistance of her loyal but undependable ally, Gonzalo, she prints three volumes of her work, but still fails to achieve the literary recognition she is convinced is her due. After her works have been sporadically published by commercial presses, Alan Swallow takes over their publication and distribution in 1961, determined to keep them in print and build an audience for them.

But her persistent dream of a landlocked boat she has to push through city streets, as well as her unpublished journals, weigh her down. Preoccupied with the necessity for ridding herself of this burden, Nin is equally disturbed at the prospect of revealing herself to a hostile or indifferent public. She imagines her identity and journal will end with exposure, or that she will be seared with "mortal radiation" with the publication of her Diary. Yet without publication of her journal, Nin denies herself the literary acclaim she has always craved, since Nin realizes by this time that her diaries and not her fiction will be her enduring achievement.

Finally in 1966, Nin's personal odyssey concluded with the publication by Harcourt Brace and favorable reception of the first volume of her edited Diary; six more volumes were published before her death in 1977. In a sense, Nin's raison d'être ceased with the publication and recognition of her Diary, so fused is the life with the book, so single-minded her aim on this journey. Having received the literary accolades, the immense self-confirmation, dreamt of for over sixty years, Nin could at last put down her pen with the publication of her Diary.

Chapter Two
The Diaries:
The Art of Seduction

To Create and in Creating to Be Created

Autobiography has been described as the "drama of a man struggling to reassemble himself in his own likeness at a certain moment of his history."[1] If we change the sex and extend the moment to a lifetime of effort, we have an apt description of Nin's Diary, which is also a drama or parable of a woman struggling to reassemble herself into a unified, coherent picture. Although the process was lifelong for Nin, the Diary as she published it[2] is a retrospective compilation of the massive diary materials which were edited and revised in Nin's later years. This Diary represents a monumental effort to "piece together the fragments" of a life, as Nin says about her autobiographical heroine in "Winter of Artifice."

"To create and in creating to be created." This phrase, authored by the French philosopher Lequier,[3] has been treated as a suitable emblem for all autobiographers, and it is certainly applicable to Nin. In devoting her life to capturing her own likeness, Nin determined the shape of her existence to some extent, and effected the composition of her portrait. She, like all autobiographers, came to know herself as she composed her own image, and that knowledge altered the person she was or would have been. She conferred a meaning on her life in the process of seeking it, creating patterns of significance by pursuing them, even deepening their dimensions by virtue of the attention devoted to them. Her life molded itself around the necessities of her art as her art responded to the motions of her life. She became the embodiment of her imagined shape.

By imagining herself into being, Nin produced an amplification of her personality, as all autobiographers do, a mythological version of self. Life turns into legend, and the challenge of the autobiographer is to fit all the pieces into the appropriate legendary shape. Though this tendency may be universal among autobiographers, in Nin's case it was accentuated by her lifelong preoccupation with the making of her portrait. For

H. G. Wells, writing his *Experiment in Autobiography* provoked questions about the artificiality of the persona he was creating, but the problem was not acute since this particular literary effort was one episode in a lifetime of productivity in many directions. For Nin, however, the autobiography was the life, leading to an unchecked propensity for self-amplification.

"It is as if I were an idol of some kind," says Nin's mouthpiece in "The Voice." "I feel I have created this personage and that I sit outside of her, lamenting because they are worshiping a sort of image, and they don't reach with simple, warm hands and touch me. It's as if I were outside this very costume, desiring and calling for simplicity, and at the same time a kind of fear compels me to continue acting" (*WA*, 147–48).[4] Nin fosters her own idolization in the Diary at the same time as she attempts to escape from its consequences. She is within the myriad costumes and masks she displays, and she is outside, peeling the layers off, to the relief, no doubt, of spectators and performer alike.

Nin attends a masquerade in Diary V in which each participant is to come dressed as his or her madness. Her costume, reproduced in the photos accompanying the text, expresses a great deal about the legend:

I wore a skin-colored leotard, leopard-fur earrings glued to the tips of my naked breasts, and a leopard-fur belt around my waist. Gil Henderson painted on my bare back a vivid jungle scene. I wore eyelashes two inches long. My hair was dusted with gold powder. My head was inside of a birdcage. From within the cage, through the open gate, I pulled out an endless roll of paper on which I had written lines from my books. The ticker tape of the unconscious. I unwound this and handed everyone a strip with a message. (133)

Her costume offers an amusing glimpse at many of the salient features of her self-created legend, beginning with the skin-colored leotard which gives the appearance rather than the reality of naked exposure. The legendary Anaïs is not so much interested in exposing her soul as in winning our admiration and love. Her inclination is to charm and seduce, and toward that end a breast may be revealed here and there, a story of erotic deviance tossed out, to create a mood propitious to an atmosphere of intimacy and receptivity. She is the *femme fatale,* a bit outdated now, with the "eyelashes two inches long," nevertheless part of an extensive cultural heritage from the Biblical Delilah to myriad film examples including Greta Garbo and Marlene Dietrich. Dusted with gold, she is the dyed blonde bombshell in disguise, and at the same time the icon—exquisite, remote, purified, already turned into art. Her head is encased in a birdcage: she is imprisoned within her legend, locked within the pages of her Diary. Bourgeois restrictions, traditional feminine stereotypes keep her encased, but she still manages to be effective within her cage. Her writing forms a link between her own delimited existence and the world outside. "Through the open gate," she sends out a "ticker tape of the unconscious." Her province is the world of dreams; she is the "mermaid with her fish-tail dipped in the unconscious." She is the guru with special messages for everyone, individually wrapped.

The mythological Nin is all these things and yet much more. She is a series of endless contradictions and dualities, as Emerson and Whitman were before her. Whitman's famous words in "Song of Myself" could be her own: "Do I contradict myself? / Very well then . . . I am large, I contain multitudes."[5] She revels in her indeterminacy and defies us to locate her in a category out of which she cannot slip. It is her elusiveness of which she is most proud, as this self-portrait from a letter in Diary IV suggests:

I am all the women in the novels, yet still another *not* in the novels. . . . Like Oscar Wilde I put only my art into my work and my genius into my life. My life is not possible to tell. I change every day, change my patterns, my concepts, my interpretations. I am a series of moods and sensations. I play a thousand roles. I weep when I find others play them for me. My real self is unknown. My work is merely an essence of this vast and deep adventure. I create a myth and a legend, a lie, a fairy tale, a magical world, and one that collapses every day and makes me feel like going the way of Virginia Woolf. . . . I am more interested in human beings than in writing, more interested in lovemaking than in writing, more interested in living than in writing. More interested in becoming a work of art than in creating one. . . . I am a writer. I would rather have been a courtesan. (176–78)

Like so many nineteenth-century women writers, Nin feels compelled to justify her desire to be both woman and artist. Her artful defense in the passage above—"I am more interested in human beings than in writing"—should be read in the context of a society which questioned the femininity of a woman not satisfied to play mother and wife. Her Diary is a long plea for acceptance and a manifestation of the need for absolution. In Diary I, Nin records a dream in which she is on a train and her journals, which are in a black valise, are stolen by someone and burned. Nin has a "great sense of injustice," and asks to have the case brought to court. She makes a speech in which she passionately defends her diaries: "In those journals you can see I was brought up in Spanish Catholicism, that my actions later are not evil; just a struggle to react against a prison. . . . Of course I am aware that I cannot talk pure legal French. I beg you to forgive my inaccuracies" (254). Like all autobiographers, she wishes to justify her life, and like nearly all women artists —at least until recently—she feels called upon to defend her creative ambition. As is the case with so many women, she craves approval and depends upon confirmation from others for her sense of self-worth. Hence she postures and does pirouettes of all sorts to gain our love and admiration. The Diary is a lengthy testimony to the tremendous need for acceptance in the woman artist and the pitfalls of that need. Wishing to be loved, Nin tends to lose sight of the arduous necessities of her craft.

Through her Diary, Nin also attempts to ward off her fear of loss and change, ultimately her fear of death, as do all autobiographers, by capturing the fleeting recollections of a lifetime. Many other occupations are more pleasurable than writing, Nin observes in Diary VI, "but *none of them give you back the life which is flowing away from us every moment*" (244). She wishes to hold onto the moment through her book, resist the ineluctable process of decay and forgetfulness, yet the prospect of life without movement or escape routes fills her with trepidation. Over and over again, she emphasizes her desire to remain fluid, mobile—"to float as words do, without roots and without watering cans"—while she remains tied to her anchor, her Diary. The legendary Nin refuses to "take root," but the lifelong diarist testifies through her immense work to her need for continuity and permanence. Such contradictions are at the heart of the autobiographer's art.

Editing: The Cone of Darkness

Nin's work is not a document of daily living, as we are accustomed to regard diaries, but a complex, voluminous autobiographical text, much of it retrospectively written and subtly altered over the course of time. Not only did Nin reconstruct her seven-volume Diary out of the more than 150 original diaries (with the help of her editor Gunther Stuhlmann), but these so-called originals were reconstructions written and rewritten days, months, and years after the events described. The Diary as we know it (excluding the early installments) is a vast collage[6] containing layer upon layer of fragments composed over the forty years of its evolution. It is impossible to be certain whether any given passage was written thirty or ten years ago, although some of these passages have all the qualities of an immediate impression, while others seem clearly to be retrospective. Nin's editor repeatedly stresses that the dates in the Diary are only approximations to indicate the flow of time. He comments on the difficulty involved in determining a precise chronology, given Nin's tendency for "later reflection on a previous event." This inclination is apparent even in *Linotte,* in which Nin rewrites the account of her arrival in New York since she felt she had not done this opening scene justice. The fiction writer was at work editing the Diary from the very start.

In a letter to the critic Maxwell Geismar included in Diary V, Nin explains that she has settled down to "round out" the Diary: "I am at work now on what I call the volume of superimpositions, which means that while I copy out volume 60, I write about the developments and conclusions which took place twenty years later" (217). Vague as this passage is, it suggests that Nin superimposed a later judgment or impression on an earlier entry. This seems to be exactly what she did in her fourth Diary in the following passage related to Gore Vidal: "Whatever Gore was with me, whatever side he showed me, was not the one he was to show in his life and in his work" (175). This superimposition of a later judgment upon an earlier experience has the effect of disrupting the aura of authenticity created by the confessional form. Nin cannot seem to resist occasionally intruding upon her text in a noticeable manner. Again, in volume IV she comments: "The story of complete freedom does not appear yet in this volume. I am still in the labyrinth, and I must be willing to get lost before I am saved" (143). Is it not disconcerting to realize in this instance that "complete freedom" is foreordained in the legend and that the material we are being offered may have been manipulated to demonstrate the appropriate conclusions?

Our uncertainty would not be so troublesome if Nin had been more consistent in her explanation of the editorial process. However, she frequently denies that she had done much alteration of her original text. In Diary VII she claims: "I have not changed anything in the Diary, only omitted, and the greater part of what was left out was repetition" (109). To add to the confusion, in *Novel of the Future,* her apologia, she explains: "I did not erase or revise, but I occasionally rewrote a description worth retelling" (153). If this distinction between revising and rewriting seems obscure, Nin's fear that revision would somehow damage the value of her

Diary helps to clarify the situation. She appears to have been convinced that her Diary would only be valuable if it were a genuine record. Henry Miller was adamant about this, in his argument for publication of the complete diaries, and his insistence may have influenced Nin. In Diary VI, in which she records her determination to edit the journals for publication, we get a clearer picture of the process involved. The fact that this volume was edited after Nin had already achieved recognition may well explain her greater frankness on this issue.[7] She muses on "how to avoid hurting or damaging people, how to reveal in such a subtle way that no explicit statement could be deduced, no facts. How to complete sketchy parts, how to eliminate weak or foggy parts" (298).

Editing seems to have involved removing fog in certain quarters and adding it in others. Sketchy portraits were clarified or "rounded out," but "no facts"—the opposite of Gradgrind in Dickens's *Hard Times* insisting upon "nothing but the facts." In defence of her avoidance of the particular or factual, Nin informs us in *Novel of the Future* that she provided full psychological portraits of everyone: "Nothing essential to a portrait was left out of the diary" (153). The psychological essence of a character was presumably offered in every case, but in such a way as to yield no certainties—especially about the life of the author, the "princess of the underground" herself, around whom there drops a heavy veil.

At the center of every autobiography, according to Roy Pascal, there is a "cone of darkness,"[8] and in Nin's case this cone contains the particulars of whom she loved, whom she married, or where her money came from, to name but three missing ingredients. It is hardly unusual for an autobiographer to omit pertinent details of his or her life. In fact, some critics have found what is left out of autobiographies to be at least as interesting as what is included. Many famous autobiographers, such as Henry Adams, have left out their wives, and many more have excluded their lovers, as H. G. Wells did. Nin omits her husband except to mention the word "husband" a few times as if in a slip of the tongue. There is no definitive identification of a lover in Nin's Diary, although Henry Miller, Gonzalo More, and Edmund Wilson are strongly suggested, and many more are unconfirmed possibilities.

Nin's reticence on the subject of love, marriage, and money is rather typical for women autobiographers. Literary critics have pointed out the "presence of absence" in women's writing—"hollows, centers, caverns within the work—places where activity that one might expect is missing."[9] Gertrude Stein's *Autobiography of Alice B. Toklas,* a masterpiece of self-promotion, is notoriously reticent on the subject of the love between Gertrude and Alice. While money is present in Virginia Woolf's *Diary,* sex is absent, as it is from her fiction—an omission Woolf regretted and saw as a defect in her work. But Woolf, like Stein and Nin were the products of Victorian child-rearing which left permanent marks on their lives, as on their literary styles. These hollows and caverns, "cones of darkness" in their work, are partly the offshoot of Victorian prudery and the assumption that women were and should remain pure, refined, angelic. The sexual frankness of Nin's mentor, D. H. Lawrence, and her intimate, Henry Miller, could not have surfaced in her Diary or fiction under the thralldom of such attitudes. Only in the underground erotica Nin wrote for a collector in the forties did she feel free to express this aspect of her nature.

Nin has explained that the reason she omitted her husband from the Diary was that he requested his exclusion. However, his presence in the posthumously published second early Diary argues against this, and in any case, it in no way accounts for the decision not to include him under a pseudonym. To understand this, the reader must consider the legend Nin wished to create in these pages of a courageous, independent woman struggling to forge her own identity and art. Those characters and scenes are included in the final version which tend to corroborate this legend. But the "cone of darkness" beneath the tale has a tendency to undermine the impact of the legend. For example, when Nin goes on her cross-country expedition through America in Diary IV, there are references to "we," but the driver of the car remains an eerie shadow figure, almost a functionary whose role it is to enable the writer to carry on her mythological journey, but not suitable for inclusion in the book. The shadows grow as the pages accumulate. We begin to wonder who these invisible accompanists are to the great symphony of Nin's life, and as they are kept in the dark, their presence looms more disturbingly. They shadow Nin's trip to Venice and to Bali, to Fez and to Mexico. Who are these unknowns and how did they affect these voyages, how did they change Nin's experience of these places? The decision to exclude them has serious consequences for the ultimate value of the Diary.

The nagging question of money also hovers over these pages: Who paid for Nin's independence and under what conditions? Was her independence an illusion, and if so, what effect did that have on her self-perception? Her general taciturnity on the subject of money is in striking contrast to Virginia Woolf's approach in her multi-volume Diary. World War I comes alive to us through Woolf's straightforward record of how much things cost, and the importance to her of being able to purchase a house through her literary proceeds is clarified through her tallying of earnings and price. In contrast, when Nin sees a house she loves in Los Angeles, it becomes hers through a mechanism so intangible as to be unreal to the reader: "My wish came true. I moved into it." This is the stuff of fairy tales: the fairy godmother waves her magic wand and the house is hers, the trip is possible, the houseboat appears. Several times throughout the Diary, the name of a maid is casually mentioned and here, too, we stop and wonder where dream and reality separate, and on what grounds Nin's independence was established. No wonder Tillie Olsen reacts in anger, asking how many servants went into making possible Nin's salons in France, New York, and California.[10]

In the later volumes, Nin attempts to be more forthright on the subject of finances, but her tone is defensive. She tells us in Diary VI that what she most wanted was a simple artist's life, but "a woman's life is always derivative in the sense that the man's profession creates the initial place, frame, atmosphere, design of the life" (14). Few readers will be totally convinced by this explanation, considering Nin's ability to create her own unique environment, beginning with her house in Louveciennes. The "legend of her wealth" is also brought up in the last two volumes, clearly a tender subject. Lawrence Durrell, Henry Miller, and Marguerite Young are all chastised for promulgating this myth, and the explanation offered is "wish fulfillment." Marguerite's fantasy of her as "Lady Bountiful" is a dream. By keeping the outline of her life so indefinite, however, Nin invited the speculation she abhorred, engendered legends over which she had more control than she cared to admit.

Structure: The Water Wheel

Nin recounts a dream in Diary VI which is a perfect image for the structure of her Diary—open-ended, an "indefinite continuum," and circular, forever turning in upon itself. In the dream, she is standing in front of a water wheel in full motion. As she watches the wheel rotate, she hears the cries for help of a little girl caught on the wheel. She is unable to move, "frozen with terror," until finally she stops the wheel and pulls the little girl out of danger. Nin analyzes the dream in terms of her obsession with *"flow";* she links the inability to move with neurosis, with a fixation on childhood ("The childhood is stuck on the wheel.") which is overcome, at least temporarily, with the release of the child at the end of the dream ("I have to rescue my childhood so that the wheel can turn harmlessly"[76].)

The water wheel is the endless book of Nin's life, and impaled on that wheel is her self, her past, and her childhood, from which she can only be released by giving up her hold on the diaries. Nin's position in relation to the little girl is also appropriate for her role within the book: she is at the hub of the wheel, immobilized by her diary-writing and her self-preoccupation, and she is on the periphery, the onlooker analyzing the meaning of the legend and rescuing her (little girl) self from destruction as well as from anonymity by her actions. She is subject and object at once, source of the action and the commentary, a closed circle, ever-in-motion, but going nowhere beyond the wheel's rotations. All images, characters, themes are like spokes emanating from her central presence. Nin's mythological personality is the most significant organizing force in the Diary. As Nin comments, "The diary was held together, was given its unity, by my being at the center" (V, 112). Everything flows back to her, the source of whatever unity and value the Diary ultimately possesses.

In describing the astrologer Conrad Moricand, in Diary II, Nin indirectly provides a picture of herself at the hub of the wheel. His monologues remind her of the "enormous wheels at the Fair carrying little cages traveling spherically . . . the illusion of a vast circular voyage. Moricand picked you up on the edge of this wheel, whirled you in space, and deposited you again without for a moment enabling you to stand any closer . . . to the hub, himself" (257–58). This same "illusion of a vast circular voyage" is created in the Diary by Nin, positioned at the hub, whirling her readers in space, without allowing them ultimately to stand any closer to the center—herself. Her voyage is illusory because in a sense it never takes place, despite the appearance of motion and time passing; both the book and the personality it contains are a dream. "Instead of writing a novel," Nin explains in Diary I, "I lie back with this book and a pen, and dream, and indulge in refractions and defractions, I can turn away from reality into the reflections and dreams it projects . . ." (333).

The Diary is Nin's dream and her mirror, her lifelong voyage and her labyrinth. These images recur like leitmotivs throughout the Diary, providing it with structure and meaning. Certain characters and themes also repeat themselves in the Diary, giving form to this vast construction—Henry and June Miller, psychoanalysis, the woman artist, the father figure. While these themes give a degree of structure to this undertaking, there is also the danger, which increases after volume

II, of a collapse into formlessness through endless repetition and fixation.

Although the Diary does not follow a precise chronology, it is broken down into seven book-length units (excluding the early Diaries) corresponding to time periods in the author's life between 1931 and 1974. Each of the seven volumes is composed of sections of varying lengths marked off by approximate dates to indicate the flow of time. The narrative is propelled along by these periodic chronological notations which remind us of the passage of time and the continuity of the text through the life of the writer.

In Diary V Nin discusses her effort to make a "riverbed for the flow of the diary so that it may not seem like a diary but an inner monologue, a series of free associations accompanying the life of several characters . . . a Joycean flow of inner consciousness" (V, 38). But Nin had difficulty achieving this effect, and the final product does not read like a "Joycean flow of inner consciousness" so much as an assemblage of diary entries in the narrator's voice. Sometimes this assemblage works as a "series of free associations"—in the first few Diaries, for example—but often it reads like an accumulation of fragments instead. Nin was aware of the danger of fragmentation in her work, calling it the "price you pay for improvisation." Nonetheless, there is truth in James Leo Herlihy's gentle reminder to Nin: "you do not organize well." This is one possible explanation for Nin's retention of the diary form, despite her desire to transcend it.

In its present form, the Diary is actually a "hybrid"[11]—part autobiography, part journal. By preserving the diary format but revising her text, Nin was able to avoid the organizational challenge of autobiography while retaining the atmosphere of intimacy and spontaneity associated with the diary. Our expectations for an autobiography are quite different from those we have for a diary. We do not expect a journal to be other than fragmented, dispersed, immersed in the particular and the immediate. In an autobiography, we are accustomed to a greater degree of organization and unity, a perceptive reconsideration of the past which imposes a certain design on the life and work. Since Nin did edit and reconstruct the original diaries, she had the opportunity to create such a design in her Diary. It is tempting to forget this fact while reading the Diary, since the author encourages our perception of the work as a spontaneous, authentic form.

"The diary is like life itself—*une oeuvre inachevée*, ever incomplete," Nin declares in Diary V. "Sometimes I would like to live long enough to terminate it in every detail, make of it a Proustian work. But to follow the life line is always of greater concern to me than the perfection of detail" (219). The structure of Nin's life-work can be seen in terms of process— the "unfinished symphony"—as Miller called it. Like her mentors, Emerson and Lawrence, Nin celebrates the notion of her life and Diary as a process of becoming: "All aspects of the self have to be lived out, like the twelve houses of the zodiac. A personality is one who has unrolled the ribbon, unfolded the petals, exposed all the layers. . . . A process of nature, growth, not the ideal" (II, 249). The water wheel, labyrinth, circular voyage, and ever-evolving circle of this description are all variations on this motif found throughout the Diary. They reveal the pattern of Nin's effort in her life-work to expose the layers of her identity, to unroll the endless ribbon of her story. Her struggle toward self-completion rather than achievement of that goal determines the structure of her Diary.

Autobiographies as a genre tend to be inconclusive, experimental, viewed as a process rather than a fixed form. Nin places her work most clearly in this tradition in the last Diary: "The very process of the diary resembles that of a painter making a series of sketches each day in preparation for a final portrait. This portrait is made only by cumulative effect because the diary never ends. As the diarist does not know the future, he reaches no conclusion, no synthesis, which is an artificial product of the intellect. The Diary is true to becoming and to continuum" (109). While Nin's assertion that the "diarist does not know the future" is not applicable to her final effort of retrospective composition, the Diary as a whole is "true to becoming and to continuum," resembling an extended series of sketches for a cumulative self-portrait.

It has been suggested that women's autobiographies as a genre tend to be "much less clearly organized, much less synthetic" than men's, closer to the immediate "records of the moment" of the diary form. Lynn Bloom and Orlee Holder place Nin's Diary within the conventions of this female autobiographical tradition characterized by "structural discontinuity" and certain common thematic concerns, such as a preoccupation with feminine physique and roles.[12] They view Virginia Woolf's definition of what she would like her diary to be as a prototype of the form: "Something loose knit, & yet not slovenly, so elastic that it will embrace any thing, solemn, slight or beautiful that comes into mind. I should like it to resemble some deep old desk, or capacious hold-all, in which one flings a mass of odds & ends without looking them through."[13]

Nin's Diary certainly fits this description of a "capacious hold-all" containing odds and ends, a "loose knit" and "elastic" structure, perhaps indicating the continuation in her Diary of a female autobiographical tradition. Unlike Woolf's Diary, however, Nin's is also at times "slovenly"—a quality Woolf warns against, and one not to be ignored in the assessment. "Henry was right," Nin comments in Diary II, "what I write is less communicable than what he writes because he has a human love of writing, of words, he takes a sensuous pleasure in writing, it is flesh and blood, whereas I have a sort of contempt for the sensuous joy of expression, I seek the meaning, the contents" (208–9). Nin's repugnance for matters of style per se is in marked contrast to Woolf's approach. Virginia Woolf's multi-volume Diary holds together as a form and maintains audience involvement despite its "structural discontinuity" because of the extraordinary beauty and intensity of her expression, her constant attentiveness to language, her use of her Diary as a sketchbook for vivid impressions of people, landscape, and events. Nin's Diary, on the contrary, lacks this same attunement to the aesthetic possibilities of "any thing, solemn, slight or beautiful." Her "loose knit" structure tends to unravel, especially in the later volumes in which the language lacks imaginative vitality and Nin's attention continues to focus on the endless revolutions of the wheel of her self.

The Art of Sincerity

Much as Nin seems to have regarded it as an article of faith that her Diary would only be valuable if a "true record," similarly she was convinced that the Diary had to be truthful and sincere. At least since Rousseau's *Confessions,* the literary public of the Western world has associated the autobiographical form with sincerity and placed great value on that attribute. Although the concepts of sincerity and truthfulness in art have been seriously called into question since that time, the craving for authenticity has if anything increased. In his book *Sincerity and Authenticity,* Lionel Trilling observes: "Society requires of us that we present ourselves as being sincere, and the most efficacious way of satisfying this demand is to see to it that we really are sincere, that we actually are what we want our community to know we are. In short, we play the role of being ourselves, we sincerely act the part of the sincere person, with the result that a judgment may be passed upon our sincerity that it is not authentic."[14] Likewise, Nin was fully cognizant of the need for sincerity in her Diary, believed she was sincere, held onto her sincerity tenaciously in her self-mythology, and in the end, will be judged at least by some as insincere.

Many readers of Nin's Diary assume, by virtue of its literary form, that the work must be more truthful, more honest than other literary forms. In the first book-length study of Nin's work, Oliver Evans remarks that Nin must have been "completely honest" in her Diary, otherwise the work could not have value.[15] In a more recent study, Bettina Knapp describes the Diary as authentic and makes no distinction between the artist and the diary re-creation of her personality.[16] Other critics have become disillusioned when they realized the artifice and illusion involved in the Diary. The problem in both instances stems from the critics' assumption that autobiography is a factual record, a sincere and authentic form, which is not actually the case. Autobiography, as much as fiction, has come to be regarded as a construction, an artifact, or an illusion. The act of composition involves a degree of falsification, of transformation and distortion of experience, no matter how truthful the autobiographer tries to be. He or she creates a fable, however determined to reproduce fact. In the case of Nin's Diary, the problem is magnified by the label "Diary" which immediately conjures up the image of an honest, daily record, which this Diary is not.

Yet it is also true that we do not respond to works labeled "autobiography" or "diary" the same as we do to those labeled "fiction," even knowing that their authenticity is illusory. This is part of the meaning of autobiography—this expectation of truthfulness, intimacy, and self-revelation—which leads to an intensification of emotional response on the part of the reader. The processes of identification and projection which take place with any literary text are accentuated with the reading of autobiography. Bruce Mazlish theorizes that autobiography is "binocular": "it offers us equal knowledge of the development and meaning of ourselves as well as of our 'other self', the writer of the autobiography."[17] Clearly some of the intensity of reaction to Nin's Diary is based on a sensation of identification and enlightenment as well as a feeling of intimate knowledge of Nin herself. However, not everyone responds to this invitation for self-exploration, and some will question the extent of Nin's self-revelation.

One of the complexities of the autobiographical form is that it can bind the reader in a relationship that allows for no disagreement. In responding to Kate Millett's autobiographical *Flying,* Elinor Langer comments that "Confession protects. By pretending we are presenting

'life,' not art, we avoid criticism. . . . The author protects herself with
the covert hope that if she says how much it hurts, no one will judge her
too harshly."[18] Nin is overt about the response she expects from sympathetic readers: "A human being who reveals himself should be treated
with the same care we accord a new type of fish, a new type of plant. . . .
We must protect him from injury if we are to share his life" (NF, 150).
Our identification and sympathy for the autobiographer can silence our
critical faculties.

  It may be partly Nin's desire for protection and an uncritical response
which leads to a repeated emphasis on the human, authentic quality of
her art. "Writing for me is not an art," she declares in Diary IV. "There
is no separation between my life and my craft, my work" (142). If there is
no separation between the two, criticism of the writing is tantamount to
personality assassination, especially after the writer's soul has been
stripped bare. In Diary II, Nin expresses her fear that putting art into her
diary "might kill its greatest quality, its naturalness. . . . No consciousness of perfection must enter the diary" (115). Yet from the
opening pages of Diary I, we are aware of reading a carefully contrived
work of art. It is this disjunction between theory and practice, between
Nin's legend of the Diary and our experience of it, that causes a
disruption of the romance of identification, a detachment which is
counter-productive to the effectiveness of the form.

  How many times does Nin tell us in the Diary that it was only because
her work was kept secret that she could be so sincere and natural! When
Gonzalo, her long-time intimate, mocks the Diary being "hidden in a
box," she responds:

I answer that the very condition of the work required its being done in darkness,
inside of a box, in secrecy. The very integrity of it depends on its secrecy. Like
the stalactite caves, it would crumble at exposure, it would lose its sincerity, the
very essence of its quality. . . . In the presence of others, I always wanted to
wear my best dress. I assumed the ultimate defenses of perfectionism, I wanted
to give only the perfect polished diamond. Inside of this shield my heart could
speak simply. But I had to promise myself secrecy or I would not have been as
spontaneous or as sincere. (III, 173)

There is an obvious discrepancy between Nin's presentation of the Diary
as her secret box and her intention to use it from the moment of its
conception as a means of communication with others, her "bridge to the
world." In Diary I Nin does not hesitate to record her attempts to get it

published, and throughout the Diary intimate friends read the book, even make suggestions for their own portraits. But the clue in this description is Nin's phrase: "I had to promise myself secrecy." Apparently, the Diary's secrecy was a fable Nin needed to tell herself in order to feel free to write. She, like nearly all women writers, suffered from an "anxiety of authorship," as Sandra Gilbert and Susan Gubar have defined it, a radical fear that she could not create, that the act of writing would isolate or destroy her.[19] Although this was probably strong motivation for emphasizing the Diary's secrecy, such emphasis also produces a certain desired effect on the reader who is made to feel privileged to engage in this intimate conversation. The reader is allowed into the hushed darkness of the cave itself, privy to its mysteries, awed into silence. Yet it is the most public of private confessionals into which we are being ushered, and an awareness of the fact may dispel some of the magic of this cave.

The art of sincerity is developed to a great degree in the Diary. Nin evolves a theory of authenticity in Diary II in response to Henry Miller and Lawrence Durrell who challenge her diary-writing habit. She validates her Diary by associating it with a particularly female form of expression. Woman's art, she says, "must be a human creation . . . different from man's abstractions." Unlike Proust who found "eternal moments in creation," she must find them in life. "My work must be the closest to the life flow. I must install myself inside of the seed, growth, mysteries. I must prove the possibility of instantaneous, immediate, spontaneous art. My art must be like a miracle. Before it goes through the conduits of the brain and becomes an abstraction, a fiction, a lie. It must be for woman, more like a personified ancient ritual. . . ." (235). Nin's Diary is, in a sense, close to the "life flow," but her writing cannot actually be considered "instantaneous, immediate, spontaneous art." The unedited early Diaries have this quality in part, but even there the writer was at work transforming and polishing "real life."

This matter of the authenticity of a work of art as a criterion of value is a complex one indeed. How exactly do we determine the authenticity of a work of art, of an autobiography such as the Diary in particular? Assuming that we are not regarding the Diary as a historically valid document, which it is not, do we measure its degree of fidelity to verifiable reality, its ability to capture a sense of "felt life"? Some readers prefer autobiographies precisely for such "slices of life," vivid glimpses of people, places, events. Boswell's *Journals* satisfy on these grounds, as do Fanny Burney's and Virginia Woolf's. Nin's Diary, in terms of the quality of observations about the world, people included, must be considered extremely uneven, with occasional sketches of brilliance, all too many lapses into the miasma of subjectivity. But let us say it is not "slices of life" we seek so much as psychological authenticity. What form must sincerity take in that case? Surely we would look for truth to feeling if not to fact, a sense of an honest attempt at self-scrutiny, in so far as that can be perceived. Certainly, a blatantly self-idealized picture of the writer destroys the sensation of psychological authenticity. Unfortunately, Nin's tendency toward self-idealization and her reluctance at times to subject her portrait to painful self-scrutiny do damage to the "sincerity" of her portrait. The art of sincerity in the Diary is a work—at least in part—of artifice, which is imperfectly realized.

The Truth of Masks

In Diary VII Nin describes being in despair because she realizes her many talks on college campuses have become theatrical performances. She appears before a group wearing a metal mask and explains that for centuries women have worn masks and played roles. Today they are unmasking themselves, she explains, and with that she removes the mask and begins to read from the Diary. The process of unmasking is not finite: beneath each successive layer stripped away, another mask appears. The Diary is a mask, as is the artist; unmasking is a form of performance as much as parading in disguise. Nin's exploration of the richness and limits of masks contributes greatly to the interest of her work.

Nin's identification of masks and unmasking with women has no doubt struck a respondent chord with contemporary women who have explored the consequences of wearing a mask of beauty,[20] of presenting a costumed, painted facade to the world. However, this preoccupation with masking and unmasking has been with us for centuries and is by no means confined to women, although they frequently have been regarded (both by themselves and by men) as the epitome of the masked personage. One of the best-known manifestations of this widespread twentieth-century obsession is Picasso's *Demoiselles d'Avignon* which depicts five women in a haunting state of fragmentation and disguise—naked yet masked, perennially unknown, yet fiercely present and exuding a primitive vitality. Nin's self-presentation in her work contains many of the same qualities, particularly the combination "naked yet masked." While she is forever confessing to us and attempting to remove her disguises, she cannot show herself before us without wearing her "best dress." She is a series of poses designed to dazzle and seduce, yet she longs to shed her artful roles and appear before us free of artifice. Her masks confine her, but they offer her a certain freedom. Emerson observed in his journal, "Many men can write better in a mask than for themselves," and Oscar Wilde, who had so much to say about the "truth of masks," observed, "Man is least himself when he talks in his own person. Give him a mask and he will tell you the truth."[21] Nin's writing is a mask which enables her to reveal herself, while maintaining her protective facade. In some ways, she can be more revelatory in the fiction than in the Diary which is such a transparent medium. The eroticism which is covert in the Diary is far more open in the fiction, in *Ladders to Fire* and *Spy in the House of Love*. In the Diary, it is primarily through the mask of *others* that Nin reveals herself—through June Miller that she enacts the *femme fatale,* through Henry Miller and Gonzalo that she projects her own anger and rebellion.

She is doubly masked, twice the performer that a male writer might feel himself to be. She wears her persona[22]—social and literary mask—throughout her writing in any case. But as a woman she must shield herself from the judgment she imagines forthcoming for her literary presumption. Like Colette, Nin makes the formation of her feminine mask part of her art, but unlike Colette, she is not willing to remove the face paint before us. Colette looks into the mirror in *The Vagabond* and is confident that what she sees beneath the mask is none other than herself: "There's no getting away from it, it really is me there behind the mask of purplish rouge, my eyes ringed with a halo of blue grease-paint beginning to melt. Can the rest of my face be going to melt also? What if nothing were to remain from my whole reflection but a streak of dyed colour stuck to the glass like a long, muddy tear?"[23] Perhaps Colette can ask these questions because she is secure in her assumption that there is an identifiable "I" beneath her performer's mask. Nin, on the other hand, has no such certainty in the Diary. She may need her mask more than Colette does to verify her reality and to gain the admiration she craves. Colette's self-acceptance does not make this admiration nearly so important.

Nin mentions in Diary III that she is profoundly moved by Isak Dinesen's story of Pellegrina in "The Dreamer." She urges Henry Miller to read the tale and he writes her back that Pellegrina describes her to a "T." "A tremendous self-idolatry," he comments. "A strange assumption that the ability to spread beauty and happiness was supremely hers. And so, to enjoy life a little more, she decides on many roles instead of

one blazing one. . . . Is this the story of what happens when one loses
one's true role in life? . . . I know that a similar thing happens to you
when you are prevented from radiating peace, joy, and munificence.
When you can't function as a resplendent, bounteous Venus you go
dead" (244). Nin's Diary is a testimony to the accuracy of Miller's
interpretation: everywhere it gives evidence of a "tremendous self-
idolatry." She wishes to be worshiped as a "resplendent, bounteous
Venus," as Pellegrina does, but she is uncomfortable with the worship
she inspires. Dinesen shows no such discomfort with the worship she
inspires from the natives in *Out of Africa;* she takes their epithet—"Lioness
Blixen"—as fitting tribute, although she is modest enough about her
dazzling accomplishments. "They all want to sanctify me," Nin complains in Diary I, "to turn me into an effigy, a myth. They want to idealize
me and pray to me, use me for consolation, comfort. Curse my image, the
image of me which faces me every day with the same over-fineness,
over-delicacy. . . ." (51). Yet she is the creator of that over-fine image, as
we discover repeatedly in the Diary, with its endless tributes to Nin's
feminine perfection.

She quotes Gonzalo who describes her as "the perfume and essence of all
things," Robert Duncan who declares that she is "enchanted and enchanting," "beautifully bewitching," Henry Miller who swoons, "How you get
to the core of everything . . . you *see* more." All of the male artists bear
witness to the perfection of her feminine mask, and she applies added
layers of paint herself. "I was never careless, inattentive, thoughtless,
indifferent, absent, or asleep," she announces proudly in Diary II (342).
She also portrays herself at times as whole, unified, as she believes the ideal
woman ought to be: "In me everything was married, love and the body,
heaven and hell, dream and action. No analytical dismemberment or
separation of elements. As a woman, I shall put together all that was
divided and give new birth to everything that was killed" (IV, 41).

Nin is the embodiment of the feminine ideal in her self-creation, the
mask of goodness and mystery at once. Here she is woman as healer,
sewing together all that is tattered and divided, sending forth new life,
not in the form of actual children, but in what she considers the more
significant shape of male artists. Perhaps her determination to be a
mother of artists is all the more fervent because the "simple human
flowering was denied her." Diary I ends with the stillbirth of Nin's child
which she says ended her hopes for the "real, human, simple, direct
motherhood." This significant deviation from the feminine ideal is not,
however, unusual for women writers, a great many of whom did not have

children in the past (George Eliot, Jane Austen, the Brontës, Virginia Woolf are examples). This does not prevent Nin from feelings of guilt for this deviation and compensatory selflessness, emphasized with great regularity in the Diary:

> To protect the poor I have denied myself voyages, luxury, clothes, comforts. I have kept only the barest necessities. I have stripped myself joyously. . . . I am born under the sign of the giver, Pisces, I will have to give even more. I have to give up visiting my father in Caux, staying in Corfu with the Durrells, Montecatini with Hélène, or Venice with my mother and Joaquin, because I have to pay for Henry's rent, Gonzalo's rent, and to feed them all. No rest. No seashore, no travel, no vacation. Voilà. No Heine's beach costume, no mountain air, no sun on the body. But I get pleasure from seeing how my children live. (II, 201)

While women writers such as George Eliot and Virginia Woolf also were somewhat enamored of this image of woman's ideal goodness, they were both more wary of the feminine stereotypes. In *Daniel Deronda,* for example, George Eliot subjects the mask of feminine perfection to close scrutiny and shows it to be wanting. Her heroine, Gwendolyn, demonstrates the pitfalls of self-idolatry. While Virginia Woolf poeticizes the feminine ideal in the shapes of Mrs. Ramsay and Mrs. Dalloway, she counterpoints these figures of integration and domestic felicity with destructive forces illustrating the fragility of this ideal. In a famous essay, she discusses the damaging Victorian ideal of the "angel in the house," an ideal which Woolf believes the woman writer must kill before she can work effectively: "She was intensely sympathetic. She was immensely charming. She was utterly unselfish. She excelled in the difficult arts of family life. She sacrificed herself daily . . . she was so constituted that she never had a mind or a wish of her own, but preferred to sympathize always with the minds and wishes of others."[24] The mask of ideal femininity which Nin wears in most of the Diary is precisely this one of the "angel in the house," with the flip side of the feminine mythology thrown in— siren, vamp, and sorceress.

Unlike Woolf, who struggles against her socially conditioned roles in her writing, Nin adapts them for the most part and even carries them further, idealizing herself as a paragon of moral virtue: "If all of us acted in unison as I act individually there would be no wars and no poverty. I have made myself personally responsible for the fate of every human being who has come my way" (II, 45). She is not only the angel in the house, but the angel in the world, the beacon of individual devotion, lighting the way to peace and harmony. Instead of diminishing over the years, this extravagant posture continues unabated until in the last Diary Nin becomes guru to the multitudes.

Periodically, however, Nin steps outside her mask of ideal goodness and provides a commentary upon it. "I subjugated my own nature so much," she tells us, "I had to live it through others, through Henry and through Gonzalo. I wanted so much to be an ideal person, wise and evolved, and of course I wasn't. I would not allow myself the freedom to be capricious, jealous, angry, selfish or irresponsible. I was . . . bound by my ideal self. . . ." (III, 304). She is inside the many costumes and masks she adapts, the mannequin removed from us by a pane of glass, and she is outside, observing the effects of her creations—though not often enough. She plays subject and object, analyst and analysand. "The basis of insincerity," she explains in Diary I after starting psychoanalysis with Dr. Allendy, "is the idealized image we hold of ourselves and wish to impose on others—an admirable image. When this is broken down by the analyst's discoveries, it is a relief because this image is always a great strain to live up to" (128).

Nin's firm conviction is that the one place where she is free of the burden of this idealized image is in the Diary. "Playing so many roles, dutiful daughter, devoted sister, mistress, protector, my father's new-found illusion, Henry's needed all-purpose friend, I had to find one place of truth, one dialogue without falsity" (I, 286). In the Diary, she tells us in Novel of the Future, she could be "depressed, angry, despairing, discouraged." She could let out her "demons." The Diary as we know it contains little of this dark side of the mask, but when it does emerge, it frequently makes for more compelling reading than the idealized visage of Anaïs that dominates the legend. Nin is at her most interesting when she describes the feelings of division which come about as a result of wearing an ideal mask: "There were always, in me, two women at least, one woman desperate and bewildered, who felt she was drowning, and another who only wanted to bring beauty, grace, and aliveness to people and who would leap into a scene, as upon a stage, conceal her true emotions because they were weaknesses, helplessness, despair, and present to the world only a smile, an eagerness, curiosity, enthusiasm, interest" (I, 270).

One of the reasons the first two Diaries are the most outstanding is that passages such as this allow us glimpses behind Nin's stylized persona. Frequently, it is through the voice of another woman character that Nin expresses her doubts and duality. In describing her friend Hélène in the Diary, Nin indirectly explores her own divided self:

She really has two faces: one at home, sewing, serious, tragic, the Catholic woman who is afraid of sinning, and the other outside, with mocking eyes, a sardonic mouth, a daring and voluptuous appearance. This aspect freezes people, or amuses them. "Which is my real self?" she asks me. Absolute duality. As there is in me. But perhaps what is frightening is that the different aspects of her personality are like women on a revolving stage, there is a wall between each rotation. If you are enclosed with one, the other does not hear you. Her heart is not there. There is only an actress, bent on seducing you. (II, 185)

Nin's acknowledgement that Hélène's duality is her own is characteristically mentioned here as an aside—in an off-stage whisper—and our attention is immediately drawn back to Hélène as if to make us forget what we have just heard. Like Sabina in *A Spy in the House of Love*, Nin is continually "lifting a corner of the veil" in a confessional fever, but then frightened at what she has said, she takes a "giant sponge" and erases what has come before. As a result, there is an aura of unreality around the text, as if we only dreamt what we read.

Often donning the mask of another character is a means of disguising the writer's own flaws, or of congratulating herself at the expense of others. Nin declares in Diary II, "I cannot bear self-deception. But Helba, Gonzalo, Henry, cannot bear the truth" (329). Reader sympathy and identification are damaged by remarks such as this which demonstrate Nin's tendency towards self-justification. "June [Miller] and I have paid with our souls for taking fantasies seriously," she admits in Diary I, "for living life as a theatre, for loving costumes and changes of selves, for wearing masks and disguises. But I know always what is real. Does June?" (I, 22). However, in another mood, she displays all the vulnerability and uncertainty about her identity previously denied:

I feel at moments I am an actress. I am a Polish countess, a Hungarian singer, an Eskimo bride, all out of novels. The men always believe in my disguises. . . . They never step behind the stage to say: "You are lying. You were lying when you sewed the hood on your coat. You are not what you seem to be." If I answer: "What am I?" it only precipitates my departure. As soon as someone denies my existence, appearance, and I am exposed as a disguised being, as a spy from another world, this other world opens its luminous jaws and engulfs me. I am here only while someone believes in me, while some human being swears to my presence and loves me." (II, 319)

Like Isak Dinesen's Pellegrina and the stereotypic woman, she is an actress who only exists as long as someone believes in her, as long as she can receive confirmation of herself in the eyes of others. She and Pellegrina fall into the void when they are asked who they are. They seek refuge in multiple roles which offer an escape from self-confrontation. The passage that appeals to Nin from Dinesen's story is the following: "If I come to think very much of what happens to one woman, that one woman, why I shall go away at once and be someone else. There are many that I can be. I will be many persons from now on." "After reading it," Nin comments in Diary III, "I felt as if my own wings were growing out again, as if I could soar again, and as if I could recover my powers of magical transpositions and disguises" (112). Dinesen inspires Nin to play quick-change artist or magician once more, as she had done in the thirties in Paris, perhaps under the influence of the surrealists. Whether as a means of transcendence or evasion, Nin readjusts her outlook in Diary III to one of "magical transpositions and disguises." When she meets the collage artist Varda in Diary IV, the mythology is revived once more:

The friendship with Varda was situated on such a level of invention, counter-invention, legend and counter-legend, poetry and counter-poetry, our talks were so far out in space, that it was like two magicians ceaselessly performing for each other. We could not rest to wipe off the perspiration, or appear for one moment as human beings, hungry, cold, or restless. Magic must predominate. Varda's attitude in life was that of a Merlin, the enchanter, who must constantly enchant and seduce, fascinate and create. Young women came constantly to him, to be metamorphosed, and it was a marvelous sight to see him create a myth: rename them, reshape them, redecorate them. . . . They were no longer ordinary women. They were myths. I was a myth, even before we met, because of *Under a Glass Bell*. (IV, 221–22)

Nin and Varda alike must constantly "enchant and seduce, fascinate and create." Much as Varda reshapes the young women who come to him, so Nin re-creates—mostly young men—in the Diary. When her "creations" are formed and successful on their own, as with Gore Vidal, Robert Duncan, James Leo Herlihy, she moves on to a new subject and witness to her magical powers. While she may identify her role as that of muse, her part is actually more active than that ancient stereotype would suggest. It is evident that Nin enjoys the fact that Varda cannot shape her as he does the young women because she is already a myth from her writing. This point is made in Diary I as well, when Nin takes pity on

June Miller for not being able to make her own portrait to protect herself from Henry's characterizations. Writing is the magical amulet that wards off the dangers of being captured by others. Nin defies the feminine stereotype in this sense: she takes pride in having the power to create herself, to name herself, and so to avoid male control and domination. She is bound by her feminine mask, and she escapes it, since it is both she and society who fashion its shape.

Autobiography as Seduction

Kenneth Burke once suggested that if "you look for a man's *burden,* you will find the principle that reveals the structure of his unburdening."[25] Nin's burden is, quite simply, her need to please, charm, "ensorcell" her audience—to use one of her favorite words. All artists have this need, but it is the extent of Nin's preoccupation with winning her audience which sets her Diary apart. It is as if Nin were constantly scrutinizing her audience from backstage, planning the performance of her writing based on that scrutiny, to the neglect at times of the patient attention to craft requisite to a good literary performance.

In order to persuade her audience that she is worthy of their admiration and unflagging devotion, she sprinkles the Diary with innumerable testimonials to her hypnotic charms. Henry Miller, Stuart Gilbert, and Lawrence Durrell are all "ensorcelled," Robert Duncan is "enchanted," and Gore Vidal is under her spell. There is a certain appeal to Nin's bewitching role in the first Diary, partly because of the novelty of her posture, but as the pages accrue, the magic begins to dissipate.

The first Diary is also more engaging because Nin exhibits the greatest candor in that volume, about her compulsive need to charm, first of all. She quotes extensively from her sessions with Dr. Allendy in which this is discussed. "Yes, everything you wear, the way you walk, sit, stand is seductive," he tells her, "and it is only people who are unsure who act constantly in a seductive manner and dress to charm" (87). Nin's inclusion of this material which explains her deep personal insecurities is bound to induce a sympathetic response in most readers. This likelihood is intensified by Nin's explanation of the origins of her insecurity. She tells Allendy and her readers that her father was preoccupied with photographing her in the nude as a child. "He always wanted me naked. All his admiration came by way of the camera. . . . How many times, in how many places, until he left us, did I sit for him for countless pictures. And it was the only time we spent together." Outside of these interludes, he never complimented or caressed her. She wonders if Dr. Allendy can actually free her of the "EYE of the father, of the eye of the camera" which she "always feared and disliked as an *exposure*. An exposure of what? Of the desire to charm, of coquettishness, of vanity, of seductiveness" (88). While confessing her "desire to charm," Nin works her magic on Allendy as well as the reader, likely to be touched by her candor and vulnerability. A few pages later, in a now-famous scene, Nin tests her seductive powers on Allendy. She confides that her lack of self-confidence is related to her fear that her breasts are too small:

Dr. Allendy: "Are they absolutely undeveloped?"

Anaïs: "No." As I flounder in my descriptions, I say: "To you, a doctor, the simplest thing is to show them to you." And I do. And then Dr. Allendy began to laugh at my fears.

Dr. Allendy: "Perfectly feminine, small but well shaped, well outlined in proportion to the rest of your figure, such a lovely figure, all you need is a few more pounds of it. You are really lovely, so much grace of movement, charm, so much breeding and finesse of line." (90–91)

Even as Allendy is charmed by this unexpected gesture suggesting exhibitionism and insecurity at once, so is the reader who is, after all, additional witness to the event. We are also disarmed from criticism since Nin provides the text as well as the commentary: "Was this quite a sincere action? Did I have to show him my breasts? Did I want to test my charm on him? Wasn't I pleased that he reacted so admiringly?" (92).

In exposing her psyche or breasts to the reader, Nin performs the same striptease her father demanded of her, only in literary form. From the inception of her journal, in fact, Nin associated writing with charming and seducing, since the diary began as a way of winning back the father's love. Nin acknowledges this in Diary VI: "Every act related to my writing was connected in me with an act of charm, seduction of my father. Every act was accompanied by guilt and retraction" (109). Nin writes in order to relieve herself of the burden of this guilt, and yet the writing reconfirms her culpability. The Diary, like the camera, has the same potentiality for exposure, for revealing the seductiveness of the writer.

The Diary is Nin's forum and her mirror before which she tests her charms and reenacts the primal drama of abandonment and repossession of the father. She must win her audience over and over again, as she must regain her father's love in Diary I, and a variety of father surrogates, such as Henry Miller, Otto Rank, and René Allendy. In the course of psychoanalysis with Dr. Allendy and later Dr. Rank, Nin begins by being enchanted with the magical healer whom she worships. Before long, however, she becomes disillusioned with the high priest after he has proven himself vulnerable to her seductive charms. Similarly, in the father-daughter legend retold in Diary I and later in "Winter of Artifice," Nin begins enraptured with her rediscovered father, but disillusioned once she is confident that she has worked her spell.

While Nin does not say incest was committed with her father, she hints at the possibility, thus fostering an erotic atmosphere throughout the Diary. This ambiance is further enhanced by the erotic fragments which appear sporadically in the journal. In the first volume, for example, Nin includes a brief scene in a whorehouse, shortly after she introduces June and Henry Miller. In a sexually explicit passage, she describes the lovemaking between two prostitutes which she and Henry witness. No comment is made upon the scene, leading the reader to wonder why the passage is included. Does it demonstrate Henry's interest in testing Nin's response to the two women (after witnessing her strong response to June)? Or is it there primarily to titillate the reader? Since Nin omits any commentary on the scene, her audience is left only with hints and guesses, which may be precisely what was intended. In a similar manner, Nin includes a lengthy description of the varieties of female orgasm in Diary II, during the period of her involvement with the Peruvian, Gonzalo. Is this meant to clue us in to her relationship with Gonzalo, or is it there to keep our interest sustained in the Diary? There is no telling; but shorn of human context, the effect is peculiarly impersonal, as disembodied as the sex in Miller's *Tropic of Cancer.*

Nin announces her intentions rather boldly in Diary III: "Ladies and Gentlemen: Just because I started in the opposite direction from the general run of adventurers, that is, I started with tragedies, not comedies, with the difficult and not the facile, it does not mean that having lived deeply and tragically I will not be able to entertain you further with more and more enticing stories of seductions, abductions and deductions. I have many surprises for you, many enchanting adventures yet to come" (277). In keeping with this aim, Nin includes several excerpts in Diary III from the erotica she wrote for a collector, published posthumously as *Delta of Venus* and *Little Birds.*[26] As if to compensate for the lack of vitality in the Diary at this point, Nin presents these erotic tidbits to the reader, often suggestive of Nin's own experience, thus encouraging a game of "deductions." She includes the tale, for example, of the young girl taken up to the attic with her two siblings to be beaten by the father. The apparent similarity between this tale and Nin's childhood experiences with her sadistic father stimulates a prurient curiosity about Nin's life which she does nothing to discourage. "There are passages in my books," she says elsewhere in this volume, "which are invitations, expectations, suspenses. Anyone reading them accurately would recognize a cue and feel, I can enter her life now. This is my clue" (174).

This is autobiography as seduction: the writer invites and excites her readers with intimate suggestions, and then vanishes behind her mask. While offering us "enticing stories of seductions, abductions and deductions," she keeps the facts and feelings of her life carefully hidden. Nin draws us into the labyrinth of her life-book, leading us on with a seductive wave of her scarf, but the closer we get to her down these winding passageways, the further she seems.

The Paper Womb

"What I have to say is really distinct from the artist and art," Nin announces in 1933, "*It is the woman who has to speak.* And it is not only the woman Anaïs who has to speak, but I who have to speak for many women. As I discover myself, I feel I am merely one of many, a symbol. . . . The mute ones of the past, the inarticulate, who took refuge behind wordless intuitions; and the women of today, all action, and copies of men. And I, in between" (I, 289). As Nin "discovers" herself in her Diary, she recognizes her importance as a symbol of a woman in transition between the old world and the new, the woman artist in search of her own voice, but dependent upon a world and language dominated by the male point of view. Her long journey in the Diary is partly defined by her effort to discern wherein she is different, to identify her female perspective. She is encouraged in this by many of those most important to her in her formative years, including Otto Rank, Henry Miller, and Lawrence Durrell, all of whom praise her Diary for its feminine insights. "We are all writing about the Womb," says Durrell, "but you *are* the *Womb*" (II, 256). In this milieu, Nin writes a short piece about her Diary which she calls her "paper womb," (later "The Labyrinth") suggesting its self-generating capacities as well as its female characteristics in her view. She develops a theory of woman's writing, partly in defense of her diary-writing habit, as "all that happens in the real womb, not in the womb, fabricated by man as a substitute. Strange that I should explore this womb of real flesh when, of all women, I seem the most idealized, the most legendary, a myth, a dream" (184).

What Nin means by writing about the "real womb" is not made entirely clear here, but elsewhere she indicates that the subject matter of woman's literature ought to be directly connected with woman's life experiences, and her style free of the artificiality and detachment Nin associates with masculine artistic forms. Nin's short story "Birth" is an excellent example of this theory, but that simple, unadorned tale of Nin's harrowing experience with a stillbirth is an unusual instance of a style and subject matter free of the artifice customarily evident in Nin's writing. The disparity between Nin's theory and practice on this issue occurs to her as well—"Strange that I should explore this womb of real flesh when, of all women, I seem the most idealized." Yet all artists must transform life in the process of creating, thereby removing art from the immediate realm of experience Nin associates with female forms. Nevertheless, other writers besides Nin have observed a preference for personal subject matter in women's art, and her exploration of this subject is provocative despite the apparent contradictions.

As a result of an intense night of discussion with Miller and Durrell, Nin comes up with an extended declaration about woman's art which is one of the highlights of Diary II. "Woman never had direct communication with God anyway," she complains, "but only through man, the priest. She never created directly except through man, was never able to create as a woman" (233). While recognizing and resenting woman's derivative stature, her problematic position as an artist in the context of a male literary tradition, Nin is reluctant to fortify her rebellious position. Instead, she equivocates, reminding woman of her dependence upon man *au fond:* "Woman does not forget . . . that everything that is born of her is planted in her. If she forgets this she is lost." She continues:

What will be marvelous to contemplate will not be her solitude but this image of woman being visited at night by man and the marvelous things she will give birth to in the morning. God alone, creating, may be a beautiful spectacle. I don't know. Man's objectivity may be an imitation of this God so detached from us and human emotion. But a woman alone creating is not a beautiful spectacle. The woman was born mother, mistress, wife, sister, she was born to represent union, communion, communication, she was born to give birth to life, and not to insanity. (234)

Nin's ambivalence about the female creative role is quite apparent in this passage. Detachment is inimical to woman's life-role, according to Nin, but the woman artist must be detached from "the myth man creates, from being created by him." She must set herself apart from male definitions, yet not alienate herself from man as "mother, mistress, wife, sister." Not surprisingly, Nin suffers from the contradictions in her viewpoint. She traps herself in the age-old mythology she wished to surpass, reducing her gender definition to biological function (woman as womb), building her legend around traditional notions of the "eternal feminine." Nin associates woman with nature, but realizes at once that her writing bears little relation to this definition. Hence she concludes that "woman is not nature only. She is the mermaid with her fish-tail dipped in the unconscious" (235). Here too she is relying on stereotypic concepts of woman as mermaid, member of the species more closely attuned to the realm of emotions and dreams. But this phrase is one of Nin's most felicitous, most appropriate to the best of her art, including *House of Incest,* in which Nin takes a deep-sea dive into her unconscious and records what she observes.

The conflicts and contradictions in Nin's definition of the woman artist do not cease in the Diary, but they do add to the richness of her journal. From *Linotte* onward, Nin struggles with her desire to fulfill herself both as woman and artist. At twelve years old, the ingenuous Anaïs comments, "perhaps I shall share my life with a man and give myself completely to my children. I prefer to give myself to my pen. . ." (64). By late adolescence, Nin does not allow herself such an admission. She has already been trained into the appropriate attitudes on maternal solicitude. From Diary I to the seventh volume, Nin exhibits protective and nurturing traits galore, to the detriment of her life as artist. She tries to cure herself of her compulsive giving to others at her own expense, but is not entirely successful from the evidence of the Diary. It appears that she is more successful at curing herself of her guilt for wishing to be adventurous.

"Adventure is pulling me out," Nin admits in Diary II, shortly after returning to Paris from her stint in New York with Rank. "When a man feels this, it is no crime, but let a woman feel this and there is an outcry. Everywhere I look I am living in a world made by man as he wants it, and I am being what man wants" (46). Nin's appetite for unconventional experience, associated with her creative role, is of course at loggerheads with traditional female behavior. Psychoanalysis helped Nin resolve the matter, according to her account. Nin announces soon thereafter that she could now abandon herself completely to the pleasure of multiple relationships, although this is not an admission Nin makes often in the

Diary. She atones for her rebellious pleasures by playing the maternal role to the hilt.

Nin is more forthcoming about her dissatisfaction with conventional female roles in the later journals, commenting in Diary V, for example, that the "African jungle seems far less dangerous than complete trust in one love, than a place where one's housework is more important than one's creativity" (237). In this volume, she observes that she was more identified with her father than her mother since she associated her mother's qualities with "submission to the *condition humaine* rather than a re-creation of it." She links "human with slavery, and the artist with the one who escapes slavery through *another life*" (130). Through her role as artist, Nin transcends the stifling limitations of traditional female roles, but her need to be loved and admired keeps her encased in the "golden cage" of her ideal woman persona.

Chapter Three
The Diaries:
Mirrors and Windows

Mirror Mirror

"Man knows himself only in so far as he knows the world," Goethe once remarked, "and becomes aware of the world only in himself, and of himself only in it. Every new object, well observed, opens a new organ in ourselves."[1] Self-knowledge, a fundamental goal of autobiographers, is the product of an interplay between the self perceived in the mirror and the world viewed outside the window. Autobiographies which omit either element generally suffer as a consequence, and Nin's Diary is no exception. Her attention is riveted on the interior life, to the near total exclusion of the world beyond the window's frame. She has no use for "ordinary reality," believing she can attain universal truths by probing inner spheres. To some extent she succeeds, but the price she pays is a diminution of the effectiveness of her art.

"I wage a constant war against reality," Nin remarks in Diary VI, "even the reality of my friends, loves, and persist in attributing to them roles in my dreams, and it is my fault if they cannot always fulfill them" (35–36). The end product of this "war against reality" is an increasing intangibility in Nin's writing, which seems suspended in a fog, stripped of social context. The mythological personality of Nin sustains our interest for the first two volumes of the Diary, which have a vitality and lyrical intensity all their own. But beyond this, the reader's interest begins to fade as Nin reverts increasingly to repetitions, denunciations of critics who fail to perceive her worth, self-pitying and seductive overtures to the reader. We pine for a breath of fresh air, a foray into the realm of the actual and out of the house of mirrors. Periodically Nin obliges, perhaps in response to criticism of the first two published volumes. She undertakes voyages to foreign parts, attempts to make her book a "journal of others."

But ultimately her Diary fails to be the monumental work Miller predicted it would be because it does not maintain a balance between the mirror and the window, between interior and exterior worlds. All Nin's windows turn out to be mirrors, and her explorations of the "real world" are compelling only in those situations in which she finds herself reflected. The abundance and variety of Nin's characters do not obviate the fact that they are nearly all reflections—shadows or doubles—of Nin herself. There are a handful of exceptions, but they do not alter the overall impression of an exclusively subjective perspective.

Ironically, the mirror-window images which proliferate in the Diary both illustrate this situation and yet counteract it, since they contribute significantly to the imaginative life of the work. The first two volumes of the Diary and the adolescent journal *Linotte* contain several passages employing reflective images which are of immense appeal. This is due partly to the vividness of the passages, as well as the resonance of these images in our cultural history. Reflective images have long been popular in the arts both in Eastern and Western culture, and have frequently been associated with women in particular. Since the infamous Queen in "Snow White" asked of the mirror, "Who's the fairest of them all?" the mirror has been linked with female vanity. Venus, the goddess of love and sexual attraction, has often been depicted in artistic renditions with a mirror held up to her face. She is the embodiment of female self-absorption, enamored of her own exquisite image, wishing to be loved rather than to love. But the image of truth has also been represented as a woman looking into a mirror, holding up her glass not to reflect herself but to see the outer world.[2] Prudence is painted looking into a glass as if it were a crystal ball, in order to see into the future. These contrasting qualities—vanity, self-absorption, as well as visionary perception—all have been associated with mirrors and women, and all find their expression in Nin's art. The mythological Nin of the Diary is Venus—as Diane Wakoski has called her[3]—entranced by her re-created image in the looking glass of her book, and she is Prudence, using her mirror to reveal penetrating insights about human nature.

Oscar Wilde made the theme of self-infatuation through the mirror of art a notorious one in his novel, *The Picture of Dorian Gray*, but the myth of Narcissus, to which the book refers, is the originator of the motif. Narcissus was a beautiful young man spellbound by his mirror image in a pool of water. Without realizing it was his own face he saw reflected there, Narcissus became fatally enamored of his own alluring image. Frustrated by his inability to reach the image he sought, he pined away and died at the sight of his own reflection, realizing only at the end the identity of his twin and the impossibility of his love. Narcissus is the symbol not only of self-adoration but of self-deception, since he comprehends only belatedly the identity of the image he seeks. Self-deception as well as self-awareness are associated with the symbolism of the mirror, and both characteristics emerge in Nin's self-presentation. The mirror gazer may easily see a false image reflected upon its surface, due to the subtle distortions produced by the mirror itself, as well as the beholder's subjective apprehension of the image in the glass. But the mirror also offers truthful reflections, confrontations with reality and the self as it exists without falsities. All of these possibilities are apparent in Nin's Diary, which is both an accurate and distorted mirror of the artist and her world.

The mirror is a magical box, seeming to contain the images reflected upon its surface, holding out the possibility of revelations beyond the glass, as in Lewis Carroll's *Through the Looking Glass.* But the fantasy of magical containment can turn into the nightmare of entrapment behind the bars of a negative impression. Nin's Diary captures the personality of the writer, locking her in its "golden cage," despite the author's efforts to remain elusive. "The transparent window of autobiography," as Steven Shapiro has remarked, "reveals things to the reader that are invisible to the autobiographer, no matter how hard he stares at the portrait-mirror he has created."[4] Autobiography is simultaneously a window opening upon the autobiographer's world and a mirror of our own. Even as the writer is framed, confined in the work, so the reader is restricted by his or her own perspective in apprehending a particular text.

The mirror can entrap or liberate its beholder; it can assist in the process of self-identification, and it can lock the gazer in a fatal self-preoccupation, as it did Narcissus. In Sylvia Plath's *The Bell Jar,* Esther Greenwood rejects the horrifying reflection of her disintegrating psyche in the glass and shatters the mirror in response. She wishes not to confront the glass, but to destroy the image it reflects. But in Margaret Atwood's *Surfacing,* the unnamed heroine chooses to reject the mirror, not in order to evade truths about herself, but to get beyond them. She is determined to probe beneath the surface of reality and personality; hence, at the crucial moment in her drastic reassessment of her identity, she turns the mirror around in her cabin so as not to be misled by surface reflections: "I must stop being in the mirror. I look for the last time at my distorted face: eyes light blue in dark-red skin, hair standing tangled out from my head, reflection intruding between my eyes and vision. Not to see myself but to see. I reverse the mirror so it's toward the wall, it no longer traps me."[5] Although Nin is not prepared to turn the mirror toward the wall—to "stop being in the mirror"—she is both liberated and entrapped by her reflection in the looking glass of her writing.

Linotte

When the young Anaïs writes in her journal, she tells us in *Linotte*, she sits by the window dreaming—not recording the details of the world observable through the pane of glass, but transported to imaginary realms. The window is a transparent medium through which the young writer cultivates the dream and contemplates her life. "I sit at the window which looks out on the ugly courtyard," she remarks, "but as a consolation I imagine that it's a countryside" (30). On the rare occasions when she makes note of the city outside the boundaries of her brownstone house, it is usually with eyes half-closed, entranced by fantasies of heroic feats or the return of her absent father.

As *Linotte* proceeds and the notion of reunion with the father dissipates, the young writer gradually shifts her writing post from the window to a position in front of three mirrors. "I am writing in front of my three mirrors," she records, "and after every other word I look at myself with surprise. Really, this time, I look like my photographs, not like myself: not dreamy, distracted, very useless, and melancholy, but simply Miss Seventeen. . ." (444). Through her "magic mirror" she replaces the external ideal which has proven so disappointing (the father) with her own ego ideal safely lodged in her secret "Inside World." The mirror of her Diary and the mirror before her eyes are devices which enable her to turn herself into a socially acceptable picture, to mold her image into one which will gain her the approbation she craves.

"I wonder what you would be like," she muses to her Diary, "if, like Pygmalion's Statue, you came to life—I think I would love you so much, because when I reread you, I notice that in spite of all my confessions, you seem always to reflect my best "self'—a completely strange person in spite of all my efforts to write nothing but the whole truth. . ." (472). Young Anaïs is becoming entranced, like Narcissus, with her reflection, improved beyond recognition. The possibilities for self-delusion and

self-adoration through her mirror art, apparent here, reach their culmination in this remarkable passage at the end of *Linotte:*

Heavens! Listen: I admit that I have lost my head, like everyone else where love
is concerned. I confess that I do not think of Browning when I look at the stars
. . . but rather of a Prince. I confess (in shame and despair) that my loveliest
dreams are like the dreams of all young girls, and not like those of a "Wise
Man." And the worst of all is that I don't find my Prince, and I am dying of
thirst for a drop of Romance, a bit of "thrill"—So—Sir Diary, I name you my
Prince of Princes and my only King on earth. I am madly in love with you—do
you want vows? words of tenderness. . . . (491)

In what could be regarded as an "apotheosis of narcissism,"[6] the young
writer turns in on her own image, declares herself infatuated with her
"magic mirror," which changes sex, nevertheless is herself that she
adores. The ordinary narcissism of the adolescent is here heightened and
intensified, partly as a result of the process of diary-keeping which
amplifies what is experienced, as it deepens the tendency toward self-
absorption. Were this proclivity not further demonstrated in the Diary,
it would not be cause for concern; however, it is one of the early
indications of a tendency toward narcissism apparent throughout the
Diary.

There is also a persistent effort at self-awareness in the Diary which at
times succeeds, other times is defeated. Although the young Anaïs is
enamored of the idealized self she has created, she recognizes it is "completely strange." Her awareness at a young age of the complex, multi-
dimensional components of this concept known as "self" is impressive. She
further demonstrates her perspicuity when, at the age of sixteen, she
records what the mirror reveals to her:

When I left home, I was powdered, painted and curled, and in the mirror I saw
Maman's image. When I came back, I was pale, serious, pensive and tired, and
my hair was disarranged, and in the mirror I saw Papa's image. It's strange, but I
have two different faces and two personalities, also very different. The face that
looks like Maman goes with the personality that is sociable, gay, full of the
pleasures of dancing and society; and the other one, that of a poet (mediocre),
goes with the personality of a philosopher (unsuccessful). You know which one I
prefer, everyone knows except the opposite sex, to whom I appear with Maman's
face. And I begin really to believe that everyone has two natures, two faces, two
personalities, but only one soul and only one conscience. It's curious, and I am

going to examine myself carefully to see which one is generally the more pleasing. (230)

Writing in her journal has given the young Nin a vantage point from which to see herself more clearly. The dichotomy she perceives in the mirror at sixteen between her external appearance and her inner aspirations, between her notions of woman and artist, continues to haunt her over the years. At this juncture, the "powdered, painted and curled" facade may dominate, but covertly through the Diary, the subversive artist within her finds expression. Through the "magic mirror" of her Diary, the young writer begins the lifelong enterprise of magnifying and confirming herself through the power and charm of her words, thereby subverting her cultural inferiority as a woman, even while reinforcing her "femininity" with her constant desire to please.

The Sheet of Light

In *The Second Sex,* Simone de Beauvoir explores the importance of the mirror to the narcissistic woman who longs to preserve an image of her self in the "motionless, silvered trap." "All the future is concentrated in that sheet of light," according to de Beauvoir, "a universe within the mirror's frame; outside these narrow limits, things are a disordered chaos; the world is reduced to this sheet of glass wherein stands resplendent an image: the Unique. Each woman, lost in her reflection, rules over space and time, alone, supreme" (594). Nin's entire Diary is, in a sense, this "sheet of glass" wherein stands resplendent Nin's own unique image. The "disordered chaos" outside this translucent container evaporates; all that remains is this reconstructed woman, "alone, supreme." But that supremacy is constantly threatened by the truths revealed in the mirror, by the revelations caught in the "silvered trap."

In an extraordinary passage in Diary II, Nin meditates on the development of her concept of self through the image of the mirror. She refers to the fact that as a child, she was without self-consciousness, as all children are, and therefore did not see herself reflected in the mirror. "The first mirror had a frame of white wood," she explains. "In it there is no Anaïs Nin, but Marie Antoinette with a white lace cap, a long black dress, standing on a pile of chairs, the chariot, riding to her beheading. No Anaïs Nin. An actress playing all the parts of characters in French history. I am Charlotte Corday plunging a knife into the tyrant Marat. I am, of course,

Joan of Arc" (181). The young woman is at first unknown, invisible to herself; she is an actress, tangible only in her impersonation of others. There is "no Anaïs Nin" she repeats, as if to emphasize the fact, only a performer, playing the parts of glamorous, heroic figures from France, the country which figured so importantly in her imaginative life. She continues by describing the first mirror in which the self appears:

The first mirror in which the self appears is very large, it is inlaid inside of a brown wood wall in the room of a brownstone house. Next to it the window pours down so strong a light that the rest of the room is not reflected in the mirror. The image of the girl who approaches it is brought into luminous relief. Against a foggy darkness, the girl of fifteen stands with frightened eyes. She is looking at her dress, a dress of shiny worn blue serge, which was fixed up for her out of an old one belonging to a cousin. It does not fit her. It is meager. It looks poor. The girl is looking at the worn shiny dark-blue serge dress with shame. It is the day she has been told in school that she is gifted for writing.

The unique, resplendent image of the self appears for the first time in the mirror in "luminous relief." The outer world disappears into "foggy darkness," while the image of the fifteen year old girl fills the "very large" mirror. The window "pours down so strong a light" that it obliterates the rest of the room. As before, this window does not offer a vantage point on the outer world, but faces inward, shedding light upon young Anaïs alone. What is illuminated is not only her centrality in this vision, but the extent of her self-doubts. The grandiosity of this larger-than-life figure is counterpoised against the deep feelings of inadequacy manifested in the girl's preoccupation with her meager dress. Clearly it is of great significance that this is the day the girl is told she is gifted for writing, but her concentration on her hand-me-down attire implies a fear that she is not capable of fulfilling the expectations now placed upon her. It also suggests the extent of her dependence upon wearing her "best dress" for the maintenance of her self-esteem.

In the final section of this mirror triptych, Nin turns from the painful revelations of the previous section to a transformed image, utilizing the mirror as a means of magical alteration rather than a source of difficult truths:

There is another mirror framed in brown wood. The girl is looking at the new dress which transfigures her. What an extraordinary change. She leans over very close to look at the humid eyes, the humid mouth, the moisture and luminousness brought about by the change of dress. She walks up very slowly to the mirror, very slowly, as if she did not want to frighten reflections away. Several times, at fifteen, she walks very slowly towards the mirror. Every girl of fifteen has put the same question to a mirror: "Am I beautiful?" The face is mask-like. It does not smile. It does not want to charm the mirror, or deceive the mirror, or flirt with it and gain a false answer. The girl is in a trance. She does not want to frighten the reflection away herself. . . . She approaches the mirror and stands very still like a statue. Immobile. Waxy. She never makes a gesture. . . . She only moves to become someone else, impersonating Sarah Bernhardt, Mélisande, *La Dame aux Camelias,* Madame Bovary, Thaïs. She is never Anaïs Nin. . . . She is decomposed before the mirror into a hundred personages, recomposed into paleness and immobility. . . . There is always the question. The mirror is not going to answer it. She will have to look for the answer in the eyes and faces of the boys who dance with her, men later, and above all the painters. (181–82)

Transfigured by her new dress, the young writer relinquishes her fears, and worries only that she will frighten away this magical vision. She is spellbound by the idol of her own creation, requiring simply that it be confirmed by others, particularly the male artists whose opinions she has been trained to value above all. What preoccupies her is the question of her beauty; she wants only a truthful answer from the mirror and from her reflection in male eyes, but the face is "masklike," as if she wishes to entrance her viewers to provoke the response she craves. Similarly, in the mirror of the Diary, Nin maintains a trancelike posture, fearful of revealing too much lest she lose the approval she requires. There too she is "decomposed into a hundred personages, recomposed into paleness and immobility." In the act of composition, Nin's self is dispersed into countless fragments, pieces of her multi-dimensional personality, but through the continuity of her book she is recomposed, reassembled as one self.

Mirror-Mad

Although the "magic mirror" of her Diary helps Nin reassemble the pieces of her life, it also reinforces her fragmentation since contained in the pages of her book are the shards of her life, representing only a partial version of her experience, sometimes distorting recollections, opening old wounds. Her continued dependence upon her journal for her self-confirmation also destines her to a dual existence since part of her must always be cut off from experience, observing and recording. The image of the broken or shattered mirror recurs in the Diary in connection with these emotions. "I am like a person walking through a mirror broken in two," Nin declares in Diary I. "I see the plot. One woman, stylish, fresh, blooming, is walking towards the Trocadéro; and the other walks into nightmares which haunt the imagination, and which I described in *House of Incest*" (255–56). While the mirror in reality and her book offers confirmation of the woman's identity and surface appeal, it also reveals the flaws in her appearance, the chinks in the armor so carefully constructed.

"I feel that an initial shock has shattered my wholeness," she explains in the first Diary, "that I am like a shattered mirror. Each piece has gone off and developed a life of its own" (103). Nin turns to the psychoanalyst Otto Rank saying she feels like a "shattered mirror." "Why a mirror?" he asks. "A mirror for others? To reflect others, or yourself living behind a mirror and unable to touch real life?" (273). Although Nin leaves these questions unanswered, the Diary tacitly answers both in the affirmative. She is behind the mirror of her life-work, presenting the public and herself with the mask of a female idol, thereby cutting herself off from a sense of her own or external reality. She is also a mirror for others in her role as woman and diarist alike, offering those who come within her range a vivid reflection of themselves, at times clarified, sometimes idealized. "I am like the crystal in which people find their mystic unity," Nin declares in Diary II. "They see their fate, their potential self . . . their secret self." (109). All autobiographies function in this way, but the reflective quality of Nin's Diary is heightened by her emphasis on this theme.

"I see you as a fine, flawless mirror," she quotes Jean Carteret as saying. "A pure mirror in which others can see themselves" (II, 165–66). This is the realm of myth: woman as pure, flawless mirror in which men, for centuries, have seen themselves enlarged and illuminated. Playing this role of mirror for others can lead to the sensation of being a "shattered mirror." "I live so intensely for the *other,*" Nin admits in Diary II, "I am so abnormally aware of others' feelings that I have fallen into the habit of lying about what I enjoy" (212). The woman constantly attuned to the needs of others, always reflecting back to them whatever they need to hear or see, risks losing her own identity. Her face disappears from the surface of the glass and in its stead are the countless others she reflects. But there is a certain safety in playing this role, since it enables the reflector to remain shielded by that "sheet of light." Nin exists behind the transparent wall of her Diary, thereby avoiding some of the harsh truths of the mirror, although periodically she emerges from behind her glass retreat and speaks without disguise. We are reminded of her

presence, only to see her dissolve through the glass like Orpheus in Cocteau's film.
This notion of her ephemerality is conveyed through the mirror image in a long, haunting passage in Diary II, part of which follows:

I liked to sit in a taxi and watch myself in the little mirror in front. I would talk to myself: I would say I need greatly to have heavy objects put on myself, on my head and feet, something like lead chains and boots. That way I would not leave the earth so easily. It is amazing with what facility I outdistance things, with what ease I float away, and soar away, and am carried thousands of miles from the spot where I stand, in such a way that I assure you I don't hear what is being said to me, I do not see the person who is there, and I am not aware of myself any more. I feel so light, so light at times, vaporous, like steam on a window which can be erased with a careless finger. . . . I made this face in the mirror, just like the face, I thought, you see sometimes on people when they are about to go insane. It is all unrelated. The eyes are not connected to the meaning of the phrase which is spoken, and neither does the expression conform to the contents of the phrase. There is a kind of panic through it all . . . I have no confidence, you see, I like to hear from people what they think of me, how I look to them, even what I have said to them. . . . (219–20)

In cultivating the legend of her evanescence, Nin removes from her own grasp a tangible identity. Her mirror art produces a disturbing dissociation of her personality, an uncertainty about the coherence of this ever-performing, ever-divided entity known as "Anaïs." Her Diary confuses with its multiple reflections, but it also anchors her, as does the taxi mirror, the sheer accumulation of words grounding her in the substantial reality of her life-book. Her Diary-anchor can be a dead weight, however, the immense volume weighing her down, preventing the development of her imaginative abilities in other forms, revealing too much when she hoped she would be "safe behind paper and ink and words."

Nin's description of her fragile connection to the real world—"like steam on a window which can be erased with a careless finger"—is echoed throughout the Diary. The window tends to be associated with the fear of being an "outcast at life's feast," as Joyce puts it. "To be inside or outside" is the nightmare for Nin, beneath the bell jar of her life-book or outside, "the pale face at the window watching from another world" (II, 240–41). Like Heathcliff and Catherine in *Wuthering Heights,* Nin pictures herself outside the window of an "eternally elusive world," nose pressed against the glass. As an adolescent, she watches a party through a neighbor's window, on the periphery of a joy which seems destined for others. Occasionally Nin announces she is now "inside," but more often she struggles against this fear of being separated by her transparent medium from the flow of life. The Diary is a window through which Nin makes contact with life, and it is a framed picture of reality reminding her of the disparity between art and life, of her inevitable separation from life as an artist.

Confined

Nin chooses to present herself at the start of her story in Diary I confined to her house in Louveciennes, staring out a window "as if hoping to obtain from this contemplation a reflection of . . . [her] inner obstacles to a full, open life" (4). Not only does this opening image suggest the writer's domestic entrapment quite vividly, but it also evokes centuries of confinement behind the window's frame for women.[7] In countless artistic renditions, women sit or stand at windows, the frame of the window clearly demarcating the limits of their experience. Martha Quest, in Doris Lessing's *Four Gated City*, seems to spend an eternity in a chair by her window, contemplating her past, unable to take action in the world at the present. Mrs. Ramsay, in Virginia Woolf's *To the Lighthouse*, also remains apart from the external world, gathering her impressions through glass.

Nin does not blame society for her condition. Although the large green iron gate she can see from her window reminds her of a "prison gate," she feels this is unjustified since she believes the obstacle is within herself. Nevertheless, when she goes to Paris too often her "mother looks disapprovingly out of her window, and does not wave good-bye" (5). Her confinement, as a comfortable, middle-class woman in France, 1931, is subtle, as are the possibilities of escape. The little gate "has a sleepy and sly air, an air of being always half open," suggesting the prospect of a way out, but only through indirect means. She can dream her way into a new life: "There are eleven windows showing between the wooden trellis covered with ivy. One shutter in the middle was put there for symmetry only, but I often dream about this mysterious room which does not exist behind the closed shutter" (4).

Her room without a view, her private storehouse of fantasies, may be her equivalent of Woolf's "room of one's own," an image of the separate space, the independence needed for the development of woman's art.[8] Behind the "closed shutter" lies the incipient woman artist to be revealed in the course of the Diary. By the end of the first volume, Nin is fully released from her confinement, having delivered a stillborn child which symbolically liberates the artist within Nin. Though she may be confined to her domestic life at the start of this drama, her dream room and the "vast wild tangled garden" behind the house imply it will not be for long. Her book on D. H. Lawrence, just completed, may offer a way out, as may the "guest of honor" for whom she has a "sense of preparation."

Guests of Honor

The first "guest of honor" appears framed in the door of the house a few pages later—Henry Miller, one of the most important and well-known characters in the Diary. Shortly thereafter, his wife June walks toward Nin "from the darkness of the garden into the light of the door," the "most beautiful woman on earth." Both facilitate Nin's release from her enclosed life in Louveciennes. They also contribute to Nin's "coming out" as an artist, since their portraits play a major role in the success of the first Diary which is Nin's best.

From the time Miller and Nin met, according to Martin's biography of Miller, June became almost a "secret code, a password, a bond, between them; he traded his notes on 'The Mansfield Woman' for Anaïs's diary observations on June."[9] Nin records a remark of Miller's in the Diary that June is "an image invented by us." She is, in a sense, their invention, their literary offspring, their means of visibility and self-recognition. She is a mirror for them both, and a means of attracting the world to them. Nin comes to see the book she wants to write *(House of Incest)* in sharing notes and observations on June with Henry, commenting in the Diary that while Miller is writing realistically about June, she feels she can be penetrated by taking the dreams, myth, fantasies of June and adding to that her "visionary perception of her unconscious self."

Her response to June even before she meets her does seem to be "visionary." "From the very first day," Nin says before they meet, "I could see that Henry, who had always lived joyously and obviously *outside*, in daylight, had been drawn into this labyrinth unwittingly by his own curiosity and love of facts. He only believed in what he saw, like a candid photographer, and he now found himself inside a row of mirrors with endless reflections and counter-reflections" (13). Although Nin's insight into Henry's response to June may be the product of retrospective contemplation of her subject, it also may be the result of an identification with this woman with whom she realizes instantly she has affinities. Nin's description of Henry's approach to the labyrinthian personality of June is a subtle presentation of his response to herself as well:

June must be like those veiled figures glimpsed turning the corner of a Moroccan street, wrapped from head to foot in white cotton, throwing to a stranger a single spark from fathomless eyes. . . . From the first day, he was trapped by what he believed to be a duel between reality and illusion. It was difficult to conquer and invade a labyrinth. . . . Certain cities of the Orient were designed to baffle the enemy by a tangle of intricate streets. For those concealed within the labyrinth, its detours were a measure of safety; for the invader, it presented an image of fearful mystery. June must have chose the labyrinth for safety. (13–14)

June represents the mythological "feminine" universe with which Nin identifies herself—mysterious, seductive, impossible to define or predict. Henry is assigned the role of "masculine" adversary in this drama, at home in the streets of the world, inclined to invade and penetrate this mystery which continues to elude him. Nin revels in June's ability to thwart this invader with the "tangle" of her stories which make distinctions between truth and illusion meaningless. So, too, Nin's Diary thwarts the reader with the "tangle" of her writing intermixing truth and fiction. Her Diary is also a labyrinth lined with mirrors, designed to conceal and protect its mysterious inhabitant from the world at large, as well as to reveal her and others through its reflective surface.

"Was she the very woman he had been seeking?" Nin asks of Henry, but she might as well have asked, "Was she the very woman I had been seeking?" Nin makes clear that she is overwhelmed by June's powerful physical presence from the time she first appears: "You are the woman I want to be. I see in you that part of me which is you" (21). While Nin is fascinated by this manifestation of her shadow self, her fantasy of the *femme fatale* she would be, she cannot help but notice disturbing resemblances to her own personality. Nin observes at once that she "lacks confidence, she craves admiration insatiably," as she admits about herself on occasion. "Her role alone preoccupies her," she comments. "She invents dramas in which she always stars. I am sure she creates genuine dramas, genuine chaos and whirlpools of feelings, but I feel that her share in it is a pose. . . . She is an actress every moment" (20), as Nin says about herself at times. The negative potentialities of her double prohibit Nin from total identification: "I who am not always sincere was astonished and repelled by her insincerity. . . . The extent of her falsity was terrifying, like an abyss" (21).

Although part of Nin identifies completely with June, another part remains detached, recognizing the artistic possibilities almost at once. This side of her is drawn powerfully to Henry, to his raw, explosive talent which she appreciates instantly and wishes to mirror in her own fashion. "My being was sundered in two by Henry and June," she says in the Diary, "in absolute discord, in profound contradiction. It is impossible for me to follow one direction, to grow in only one direction" (51). Part of the conflict is between the woman and the artist: the woman longs for the ideal beauty of June, but fears the destructive aspects of her personality; the artist wants the talent and drive of Henry, but fears the loss of her "femininity."

Nin informs us that June does not "reach the same sexual center" of her as man does, but clearly she is stirred deeply. Gradually, however, June's drug addiction, compulsive lying, and lesbianism become apparent, as does Nin's desire to dissociate herself from these tendencies. She records the sordid aspects of June's behavior. Instead of June being the "most beautiful woman on earth," she turns into a gold digger and a drunk, collapsing in a final scene into a heap of drunken vomit. From an overinflated view of June, Nin gradually shifts to a perception of her as a helpless child, "her face blurred behind the taxi window, a tormented, hungry face, unsure of love, frightened, struggling desperately to wield power through mystery" (137). June no longer exerts her magnetic powers over Nin, now safely distanced from her double, notebook firmly in place, recording all the flaws, looking on with maternal solicitude. She feels pity for this woman who, through the glass of the taxi, "looked like a woman drowning."

Henry Miller, according to the Diary account, never presents quite the same dangerous possibilities as June, although he also becomes a negative force Nin must battle. "I feel that Henry undermines my self-confidence, sows nothing but doubts in me" (253), she explains to Lawrence Durrell in Diary II, but she never dramatizes the process of erosion of her esteem by Miller. Henry questions her diary-writing habit, as nearly everyone does, but he also takes it seriously, as is evidenced by his panegyric to her great confessional. They each function as mirrors for the other, offering an image of potential literary greatness to the other's eyes. Nin claims to have believed in Miller's talent far more than her own, but this may have been a "feminine" wile.

They also serve as windows for each other, opening up previously unknown worlds enriching to their lives and art. To Miller, Nin offers access to the world of his unconscious. "In you was the vivification, the living example," he wrote her, "the guide who conducted me through the labyrinth of self to unravel the riddle of myself, to come to the mysteries."[10] Henry's responsiveness to Nin's psychological probings seems to have changed, however, over the years. In Diary II, Nin complains of Henry's disinterest in "insight or understanding." "Henry is not reaching for depth but for quantity," she comments. His enlarged world is "empty of feeling, humanity, drama" (258).

Initially, Miller offers Nin a release from the constrictions of her life. He brings her "into the streets," as she phrases it several times, suggesting an expansion of her viewpoint, along with a possible degradation. Through Miller, Nin is exposed to ordinary life, encouraged to incorporate the everyday into her expression. "We are part of the street," she declares in Diary I. "It is not Henry, Fred, and I eating, but the street full of people eating, talking, drinking. It is the whole world eating, drinking and talking. We are eating also the noises of the street: the voices, the automobiles, the cries of the vendors, children's cries, the cooing of doves, the flutter of pigeons' wings, the barking of dogs. We are all fused" (116). In the spirit of Miller and Whitman before him, Nin embraces every object in sight—indiscriminate, at ease, without self-consciousness. But the mood is temporary. Counterpoised against this fusion with the masses is Nin's abhorrence of the ordinary, similar to her father's. Part of the drama of Diary I is the pull between Henry's bohemian artist's life "in the streets" and her father's elegant, aesthetic life shuttered from exposure. For the time being, Miller dominates, providing nourishment for the hungry young artist. Her hunger is palpable here, as is her excess response to its appeasement. She must consume everything in sight, in compensation for years of life behind the window.

In Nin's version of this relationship, far more emphasis is placed on her role in re-creating Miller as artist than on his role in assisting at her creative birth. Nin's gift of her typewriter to Miller, recorded in Diary I, is an example. This self-sacrificing deed has won Nin much sympathy and Miller a good deal of wrath for demanding so much of Nin and forcing her to abdicate her own creative work in favor of his. It should be kept in mind, however, that Nin preferred the dramatization of her self-abnegating role, as is evident throughout the Diary. This act of giving her typewriter to Henry was more the grand gesture than a deed of great self-sacrifice. The typewriter was soon replaced, and Henry does not seem to have demanded the gift, as this passage from a letter of his indicates: "I appreciate very deeply your lending me your own machine," he writes. "Does it mean, however, that you won't have one yourself?"[11]

He goes on to explain that someone else has also offered to lend him a typewriter so there is no need for her to deny herself. This response, of course, is not included in the Diary, suggesting not purposeful deceit on Nin's part, but the intensification of her "feminine" role in the Diary.

Jay Martin documents the fact, in his biography of Miller, that Henry followed Anaïs to New York when she went to assist Rank in his work and took over some of the overflow of her patients for a time.[12] Not only is this not included in Diary II, but Henry is practically invisible during this segment of Nin's story. Perhaps Henry's participation is excluded from the book because it would have undercut the glamor of Nin's role as analyst, in addition to making clear the emotional as well as aesthetic bonds in this relationship.

Although an indeterminate amount of material is left out of Nin's published version of this relationship, by virtue of Nin's editorial decisions and Miller's personal request, a pattern emerges over the course of the journal. In Diary II, after Miller receives critical acclaim for *Tropic of Cancer,* Nin's portrait of him takes on an increasingly negative aspect. She seems to lose interest as her subjects emerge successfully from the creative cauldron. The unstated rivalry between them appears to be an element in the darkening of Miller's portrait over the years. Nin could not help but be resentful at the contrast in their literary fortunes up until the publication of her Diaries in the 1960s. While this is not openly discussed, her bitterness occasionally surfaces. She complains in Diary II that Henry is "surrounded by admiring disciples who flatter him and do not question his opinions" (264). The Henry she first knew, she tells us, was "humble and unsure," whereas the "Henry of today is self-assured and slightly megalomaniacal. Always talking about China and wisdom. . ." (273). Henry's penchant for severing human connections during writing marathons seems to have irked Anaïs, as well as his posture of benign acceptance, passivity, resignation which becomes more pronounced as the world around them threatens to collapse. At the same time, his growing obsession with writing about sex bitterly disappoints Nin. After reading over *Tropic of Capricorn,* she concludes, "Instead of investing each woman with a different face, he takes pleasure in reducing all women to a biological aperture" (260). As to how Nin might have dealt personally with this orientation, the answer is not to be found in the Diary. Instead, Nin puts us off the track with comments such as the following: "The only personal, individual experience he had was June, because she tormented him, and was thus finally able to distinguish herself from the ocean of woman" (260). Nin's relationship with Miller was far deeper than we might be led to believe from this statement, but their primary impact on each other probably was a literary matter. In any case, Miller fades from view after the Paris Diaries, with occasional appearances thereafter, mostly in epistolary form.

The Deforming Mirror

The mirror Nin holds up to the many characters parading through the pages of her book is not always the "fine, flawless mirror" Jean Carteret believed it to be. More often, it is a magnifying glass, alternately enlarging and then diminishing the objects upon which it settles, as in the case of June Miller. Nin's determination to make her book worthy, combined with her penchant for romanticization leads to an idealization of many of her characters followed by bitter disillusionment. Even in adolescence, Nin was aware of this problem, as she reveals in *Linotte:*

It's strange how often I was wrong in my judgment of people. I always begin by thinking they are angels—and the ending is sad. It is as though I were walking through an endless gallery, with little idols on the right and on the left, each one on a pedestal. I stop before each one, and at first glance, I cry out: "What a beautiful idol!" And when I study it, I think it must be carved in gold. Then suddenly it falls and breaks into little pieces, and when I bend down to take a closer look, I find only pieces of painted clay. Then I turn away and look at another one. It falls at my feet, a little pile of clay. And so on until all the idols are broken. Behind me, the gallery is a sad spectacle of ruin; before me are many more idols, shining and drawing me on. At the end of the gallery is an immense, wonderful statue of pure gold. As I move forward, watching the false treasures fall at my feet, I draw near the statue and recognize its value. (396)

The gallery which is a "sad spectacle of ruin" is the Diary, and the only unbroken statue, the "immense, wonderful statue of pure gold" is of course the ideal Nin persona. As for the broken statues, Robert Duncan, Gore Vidal, and James Leo Herlihy are three of the better known examples.

When Nin first meets the young poet, Robert Duncan, in Diary III, he is a magical figure out of fairy tales, a medium with his flowing talk, who is drawn into her "mesmerist's chamber." The two of them share an idyllic intimacy for a time, exchanging diaries, enjoying the "rich spectacle" of their multiple roles. Nin is not specific about these roles, any more than she is about Duncan as a character. He is covered with the customary vagueness Nin favors, "wrapped in a nebula of chaos," as she puts it. He is one of several "transparent children" with whom Nin surrounds herself in the third and fourth volumes, enjoying the maternal role she plays and the compliments which are profuse from these young writers. "It is your life itself which will become monumental," Duncan writes. "The writing is only a record, a vicarious record of that creation . . ." (III, 98). Before long, however, Nin tires of her role as caretaker and muse. She complains of continual demands by Duncan and her other "children" on her time and funds. Nin retells the story of their first meeting, describing him this time as an incessant monologuist instead of a "strikingly beautiful poet." However, she recognizes at one point that she is casting her own reflection on him, as she is on the actress, Luise Rainer, with whom she becomes similarly intimate and then disillusioned: "I discovered the coldness in Robert at the same time as I discovered it in Luise. I cast my own warmth around me and it is reflected in others. I believe in this warmth and humanity and suddenly find it is not there. Nothing repels me more than absence of feeling" (III, 163). Although Nin recognizes the projection involved in her response to Duncan, she is more concerned with presenting herself in the best light and gaining our sympathy, than in exploring her subjectivity.

In Diary IV, it is Gore Vidal who plays the role Duncan does in Diary III. When Nin first meets him, he is the slender, cool-eyed descendent of "Troubadour Vidal," but before long he is an arrogant, power-hungry and perverse manipulator of human beings. What particularly embitters Nin is his book, *The City and the Pillar* (his third published novel) which contains a biting portrait of an older woman Nin interprets as based on herself. After this, Nin's negativism towards Vidal is unrelenting, leading her to assert that she is ashamed to have known him. Although she realizes (and her trusted friend, Frances Field, confirms the fact) that she might have imagined the Vidal she thought she knew, she prefers her dreamed version of people to the reality she continues to devalue.

James Leo Herlihy, author of *Midnight Cowboy*, fares better in Diary V and VI, partly because Nin attempts a greater degree of objectivity during this time period. We learn more details about Herlihy's background and appearance, but the focus of attention with him, as the others, tends to be on Nin herself. The lengthy correspondence between them enriches Nin's Diary, although it frequently serves to confirm Nin's self-importance ("You are mediocrity's executioner," he writes). As long as Herlihy is keeping a diary as Nin suggests, things seem to run smoothly between them. But when he questions the journal form, and his work gains in popularity and recognition, Nin grows dissatisfied.

They have a rift over his first book, *All Fall Down,* which Nin dislikes because the characters are such "limited, shrunken, inarticulate, almost subnormal people . . . mental dwarfs" (VI, 218). Herlihy responds angrily: "Is there such a thing on earth as a human being of so little value that he is outside of a writer's focus . . ." (219). He notes that Nin has always rejected the ordinary, "oatmeal" people as she calls them, leading, he suggests, to a "kind of blindness, tone deafness, to certain other worlds." It turns out that the characters Nin lambasted were based on members of Herlihy's family. Not surprisingly, the friendship peters out shortly thereafter, with Nin's former "spiritual son" tossed "out of the nest for good. No family resemblance."

In her portrait of the literary critic, Edmund Wilson, Nin also begins by unnaturally enlarging her subject, although in this case to an authority figure out of childhood nightmares. He is the "enemy," the "man," a "dictator up there on his *New Yorker* throne." We hear nothing of his views, get no sense of his intellectual range, but instead, of Nin's success in once again casting her spell on a potentially strong protagonist of the paternal order. She complains about his ossification, but does not hesitate to quote extensively from his admiring reviews of her books. After realizing once again it was not Wilson she sketched but her "image of reality," Nin tumbles down the well with Alice, describing a Wonderland view of immensely enlarged trucks which make her feel miniscule, overwhelmed by feelings of vulnerability and helplessness. This paternal figure has reduced her perspective to a child's, as has happened before, and as she believes we are all susceptible to experiencing:

Enter this laboratory of the soul where incidents are refracted into a diary, dissected to prove that everyone of us carries a deforming mirror where he sees himself too small or too large, too fat or too thin, even Henry, who believes himself so free, blithe, and unscarred. Enter here where one discovers that destiny can be directed, that one does not need to remain in bondage to the first wax imprint made on childhood sensibilities. One need not be branded by the first pattern. Once the deforming mirror is smashed, there is the possibility of wholeness; there is a possibility of joy. (I, 105)

Nin's intention to smash the deforming mirror remains an admirable goal not fully realized in the course of the Diary. But in the sixth volume, partly as a result of analysis with Dr. Inge Bogner, Nin comes to grips, to some extent, with the subjectivity of her portraits. She attends meetings for people interested in the ideas of Rank and Artaud and comes away from both disturbed at all she had left out of her portraits. With Artaud, she "felt suddenly that the very personal quality of the diary . . . was incomplete." She wanted to "see people from all angles" (277–78). Nin returns to her portraits of Artaud and Rank, attempting to round out both with more attention to their ideas. It is impossible to ascertain what changes might have been made at this stage, but both are vivid, if incomplete, renderings in the final Diary form.

Perhaps it was at this stage that Nin sketched the great scene in Diary I of Artaud's theater performance at the Sorbonne in which he does a reenactment of the plague, screaming, delirious, miming his own death and crucifixion. But even here, the highlight of the scene comes at the end when he walks straight up to Nin in the nearly empty hall and kisses her hand. To be kissed by Artaud, Nin tells us in Diary I, "was to be drawn towards death, towards insanity." Nin's brief flirtation with this surrealist madman (and important innovator in the theater) reaches a nervous climax when she arrives at his apartment "dressed in black, red, and steel, like a warrior" to defend herself against possession. The fact that Nin would dress symbolically for the occasion overwhelms Artaud who is nevertheless distrustful of this "all-powerful temptress." This peculiar intimacy ends badly when Nin returns from a stay with her father in the south of France to find Artaud suspicious that an "abomination" has occurred between daughter and father. From an interesting case study, Artaud is converted at this moment to an "outraged castrated monk," never to be heard from again outside the walls of the asylum.

Nin's deforming mirror adversely affects both her self-portrait and her portraits of others in the Diary, making them all vulnerable to unnatural enlargement and then diminishment, calling into question the clarity of Nin's perceptions as a whole. Despite her best intentions, Nin does not "see people from all angles." Of course no writer possibly can, but the degree of Nin's subjectivity seriously hampers her endeavor. While she wishes her Diary to be a "fine, flawless mirror" of self and others, Nin's vision is distorted by her own immense defenses and needs. Her reluctance to see others for what they are is connected with her general distrust of the ordinary, the real. This, too, has negative consequences for her Diary since she has little interest in capturing the particular, complex reality of a given human being. Her disinterest in the specifics of gesture, speech, or background leads to an eradication of distinctions between characters. They all begin to sound alike after a certain number of pages, especially given Nin's penchant for vague, abstract language.

Renate Druks, one of Nin's favorite characters from the later Diaries (fictionalized in *Collages*) with whom she never becomes disenchanted, illustrates the problem. When Nin first meets Renate and her companion, she comments that they could "easily become 'characters' in the diary." Despite the fair amount of space devoted to Renate, she never does become real, not surprisingly after this introductory remark. Utilizing some of her favorite expressions, Nin describes her as "fluid as mercury," in a continual "state of natural intoxication," with her "vertiginous conversation." Out of such abstractions, we can hardly construct a tangible picture. Nin offers no illustrative dialogue, anymore than she does with Herlihy who has "jazz speech" or Duncan with his mesmerizing flow. Renate writes Nin that she sometimes feels Nin invented her. "But how the role fits," she exclaims, willing object of Nin's magic mirror. Renate definitely contributes to the vitality of Diary V, but as a shadow or stand-in for Nin, not as an entity herself. The costume parties she stages, we suspect for Diary readers as much as for the participants, are delightful reading but as artificial as the depiction of her personality. Looking for "characters" lifelong for her book, Nin failed to produce more than a handful of convincing portraits.

Through the Window

We have already seen in *Linotte* how the young Anaïs half-closed her eyes when positioned in front of her window, intent on imagining rather than perceiving. In the second early Diary, despite several passages testifying to the young writer's awareness of the outer world, she describes herself "as though lost in a dense fog." Only beautiful things capture her attention, she explains, but "people's voices" and the "real world" are far away. The "dense fog" never completely lifts, anymore than her preference for the beautiful changes. She continues to keep her eyes half-closed in order not to see the ugliness in the universe (with rare exceptions, such as her trip to Fez). Yet she believes the hallmark of her Diary is her visionary perception, her role as "EYE, eye of vision," the crystal clear mirror. Hence she boasts in Diary II that she cannot close her eyes to things or remain blind as Henry Miller does. She wishes to see—but only the beautiful; when the "monster" of ordinary or ugly reality rears its head, she scrambles through her labyrinth looking for the nearest exit.

"I am at home in the marvelous," she exults in Diary II. "I am uncomfortable and paralyzed in the common" (186). Nin's attention to the world outside the self in the Diary is determined by her view that ordinary reality untransmuted by the imagination is either dangerous or unworthy. Although Nin's attitude undergoes a certain modification in the fifth and sixth volumes, partly in response to analysis with Dr. Bogner (and perhaps to critical feedback on the first few Diaries), she continues to defend her penchant for the marvelous. But as Wallace Stevens points out, "The imagination loses vitality as it ceases to adhere to what is real."[13] This is precisely what happens in the Diary.

Nin stands by the open window in her bedroom in Diary I and records what she observes:

> I have just stood before the open window of my bedroom and I have breathed in deeply all the honeysuckle-perfumed air, the sunshine, the snowdrops of winter, the crocuses of spring, the primroses, the crooning pigeons, the trills of the birds, the entire procession of soft winds and cool smells, of frail colors and petal-textured skies, the knotted snake greys of old vine roots, the vertical shoots of young branches, the dank smell of old leaves, of wet earth, of torn roots, and fresh-cut grass, winter, summer, and fall, sunrises and sunsets, storms and lulls, wheat and chestnuts, wild strawberries and wild roses, violets and damp logs, burnt fields and new poppies. (68)

Rather than noting the particulars of the view (in however imaginative a form), Nin closes her eyes, as she did in *Linotte,* and conjures up a catalog of the seasons, leaving the reader with no picture formed, but a lengthy, incongruous list instead. Compare this to Katherine Mansfield's impressions from the window in her *Journal*:

> I went to J's room and looked through the window. It was evening, with little light, and what was there very soft—the Freak Hour when people never seem to be quite in focus. I watched a man walking up and down the road—and he looked like a fly walking up a wall—and some men straining up with a barrow—all bottoms and feet. In the house opposite, at a ground-floor window, heavily barred, sat a little dark girl in a grey shawl reading a book. Her hair was parted down the middle: she had a small, oval face. She was perfectly charming, so set in the window with the shining white of the book. I felt a sort of Spanish infatuation. . . .[14]

Mansfield creates an arresting picture here because of the vivid, haunting details of her description of the little girl, and her fanciful depiction of the man who "looked like a fly walking up a wall." There is a dream-like quality throughout—"men straining up with a barrow—all bottoms and

feet"—developed fully in Mansfield's *Journal* along with lengthy records
of her dreams. Despite Nin's many references to dreams and their importance, there is a surprising lack of dream material or imaginative flights in
the Diary. Evidently, Mansfield, like Woolf, used her diary as a sketchbook, to sharpen her impressions, perfect her craft, in a way clearly felt
here and absent, for the most part, from Nin's Diary.

For Nin, language is a means to an end, and the end is the exploration of
the labyrinth of her inner life. But the question remains: how does one best
capture the inner life? Virginia Woolf contemplates this issue in her Diary
and concludes, "the truth is, one can't write directly about the soul.
Looked at, it vanishes: but look at the ceiling, at Grizzle, at the cheaper
beasts in the Zoo which are exposed to walkers in Regents Park, & the soul
slips in."[15] Partly because Nin looks too long in the mirror, and not
closely enough at the surrounding world, the "soul" tends to vanish from
her work. It "slips in" from time to time, to be sure, usually on those
occasions when Nin finds a reflective pool to contemplate.

One of the most effective pieces of writing in the Diary is to be found in
just such a reflective pool—Nin's visit to Fez, Morocco in Diary II, which
turns out to be an image of her inner self. "One always, sooner or later,
comes upon a city which is an image of one's inner cities," Nin declares.
"This may explain my fascination for it. Wearing a veil, full and inexhaus-
tible, labyrinthian, so rich and variable I myself get lost. Passion for
mystery, the unknown, and for the infinite, the uncharted" (74). With
marvelous effect, Nin describes a visit to Fatima, queen of the prostitutes,
with her "straight patrician nose, enormous black velvet eyes, tawny
smooth skin, full but firm, and the usual Arabian attributes of several folds
of stomach, several chins. . . . She was both queenly and magnificent,
opulent, and voluptuous. She was dressed in a wedding costume, a pink
chiffon dress embroidered with gold sequins . . . (74–75). The two of
them sit facing each other "cross-legged on vast pillows." Wine, incense,
and music are provided to increase the writer's excitation. The handsome
bodyguard translates Fatima's compliments on Nin's beauty. A fight
ensues outside and breaks into their drugged repose, but the musicians
simply play louder so as not to spoil Nin's pleasure. After a few hours, she
leaves and returns to her hotel through the quarters of the city, noting the
foulness of the air, the ugliness of faces, despite her usual aversion to such
unpleasant details.

In another memorable scene, Nin joins the Arab women in their baths,
recording the process of undressing, lengthy for the Arab women and rich
with significance for Nin. They wore so many skirts "which looked like

bandages, so much white muslin, linen, cotton to unroll, unfold, and fold again. . . . I felt they could never be really naked, that all this they wore must cling to them forever, grow with their bodies" (77). She joins them in the communal ritual of the bath, noting the beauty of the women's faces, with heads which "rose from formless masses of flesh, heaving like plants in the sea, swelling, swaying, falling, the breasts like sea anemones, floating, the stomachs of perpetually pregnant women, the legs like pillows, the backs like cushions, the hips with furrows like a mattress" (79). When the unsanitary soap is passed around, Nin removes herself from the baths. The women surround her, amazed at her lack of flesh, her tiny waist. They soap her with tenderness, talk with "volubility" while transmitting "messages of all kinds with their eyes, smiles, talk." An old woman douses Nin repeatedly with water, the final stage in this ritual female cleansing which leaves her feeling reborn.

After Nin returns from her visit to Fez, she seems to make a determined effort to record events from the rapidly disintegrating world around her (it is 1936). She alludes to strikes—the first such reference in the Diary, but explains that she clings to the world of the artist because the "other is full of horror" and she can see "no remedy for it" (83). Her involvement with the Peruvian radical, Gonzalo, brings her momentarily into contact with the political activities surrounding the Spanish Civil War, but Nin's coverage of this issue does more harm than complete avoidance would have. She declares at one point that the "death of the Republicans in Spain" wounds her "like the death of flesh" she loves, continuing in the following sentence to boast: "I am sensitive to every face I see in the street, every leaf, every cloud, every form of love, and is it the universal one waking in me?" (92). Similarly, she describes a Spanish Civil War veteran she hears coughing next to Gonzalo's political office. "His coughing fits hurt me," she exclaims, but proceeds in the following paragraph, without apparent awareness of the contrast, "I will never be able to describe the states of dazzlement, the trances, the ecstasies produced in me by love-making" (251). Nin's credibility and her reader's involvement are both disrupted by such careless juxtapositions.

After her relinquishment of the houseboat and forced departure from Paris to New York in 1939, Nin retreats even more to her inner world, as the Second World War rages. Her one comment about Hitler in Diary III consists of the following: "If people knew more about psychology they would have recognized in Hitler a psychotic killer. Nations are neurotic, and leaders can be psychotic" (49). The outer world which had briefly peeped through the Diary under Gonzalo's influence in volume II evaporates again, only to reappear in Diary IV when Nin decides to take a cross-country tour of America, following Miller's example (recorded in his *Air-Conditioned Nightmare*).

"After the city I became aware of how rarely I lived the moods of the sky, how rarely I had a clear view of it" (198), Nin admits at the start of this expedition, but unfortunately, a clear view is not provided for the duration of this trip. On the road from Weeks Hall's mansion, "The Shadows," in southwestern Louisiana, to New Orleans, Nin mentions the blue and purple mountains, but there are no mountains in this state, nor is there a seashore in New Orleans, despite Nin's reference to the same. Nin's vision is blurred, as her style is increasingly haphazard, her language repetitive. "The Shadows" is described as follows: "Pools with moss-green bottoms, peacocks, statues, noble stairs, noble columns, noble doors, noble windows. . ." (200). Nin's penchant for repetitiveness in fact seems to worsen with the years. The word "sex" gets repeated five times consecutively in Diary III (111), "joy" nine times in IV (24), and "rhythm" three in the same volume. It is as if Nin were hypnotized by her Diary, long ago having discarded matters of style and preoccupied only with treading her labyrinthian path to the end.

However, portions of Nin's cross-country trip are most effective, such as her portraits of Lloyd Wright and Varda. Again, in the fifth volume, despite uneven, flat, repetitive prose in places, Nin's description of Renate's parties, a Fourth of July event on East Hampton, trips to Mexico and Paris are well-rendered. "I wanted to live on the outside," Nin explains in this volume, "to see how it was to stay outside and never re-enter the cave of the interior life" (63). Toward this end, she includes several fines scenes in Diary VI as well, including a description of a Tinguely happening at the Museum of Modern Art, of the Watts Tower in Los Angeles, and another trip to Europe. But these are merely interludes in a journey which from the start has been locked in the "cave of the interior life."

The Ultimate Mirror

Nin's effort to "stay on the outside" in Diary V is probably linked with the deaths of both her parents which occurred during this time period. Prior to this point, Nin's Diary was noticeable for its near total exclusion of the topic of death, but with the passing away of her parents, Nin finally struggles to come to grips with this issue. She writes simply and eloquently of her complex, ambivalent feelings for her mother, a subject also not discussed previously in the Diary. Her favorite image of her mother, singing spontaneously at seventy with an Irish carpenter building Nin bookcases, is a touching conclusion to this delicate and forthright portrait (see Chapter 1).

Her account of her father's death is in stark contrast to this; while Nin has ambivalent feelings about her mother's death, she arrives at a certain accommodation by the end of her meditation on this subject. But with her father, the feelings are determinedly unresolved: "I cannot accept his death. It will never heal. Because it was an incomplete, an aborted, an unfulfillable relationship" (51). The extent of her identification with her father makes a resolution of her feelings that much more difficult. Perhaps she wishes to "stay on the outside" to forget the fact that in the end, "all photographs but those of himself . . . were hung around the walls" (52).

From the time of Nin's reunion with her father, recorded in Diary I (and in *Winter of Artifice*), it is clear their relationship was one of identical twins, alternately infatuated and appalled at their mirror likeness. When Nin first sees her father after a twenty-year hiatus, she says both of them were "looking into mirrors, to catch reflections of blood twinship" (207). "Every narcissist dreams of a twin," she observes, but this dream turns into a nightmare as Nin realizes the pitfalls of her identification, as she did with June Miller. "He, too, suffers from romanticism, quixoticism, cynicism, naïveté, cruelty, schizophrenia, multiplicity of selves, *dédoublement,* and is bewildered as to how to make a synthesis" (208). Nin attempts to separate herself from her father, as she did with June—"*I had always lived not to be my father*"—but again, she becomes entangled in her identification and it takes time for her to extricate herself. The stages of her strange courtship and then alienation from her father are explored in the first Diary and "Winter of Artifice" with the usual mixture of mystery and innuendo (see Chapter 5). Nin seems to be healed of this haunting relationship by Otto Rank, who reassures her by placing her obsession in a mythic context. She is cured by transferring her affections to a less dangerous paternal figure.

Nevertheless, the ailment continues—the mirror disease or narcissism which she recognizes in her father and which pervades the Diary. It is tolerable in the first few volumes, but less so as the pages accumulate. Nin becomes increasingly absorbed after the Paris Diaries in her pursuit of recognition and frustrated at the resistance, hostility to her fiction she encounters. She addresses us with impatience and self-pity in Diary III: "Let me be published. By not publishing me you seal my lips, you entomb me, you deny my existence. I love the world, and you throw me

back into my small personal world" (115). As if to compensate for her
lack of success, she includes endless fan letters in the Diary, populates
her life-book with admirers, devotees at the shrine who testify to her
legendary character. Those who fail to express unqualified admiration,
who dare to suggest inadequacies in the writing, risk censure and
disinheritance from Nin's literary kingdom.[16]

Nin's inclination to use her Diary as a form for special pleading reaches
its ultimate expression in the last Diary, the record of her final years
when illness and celebrity were both hers in abundance. This Diary is
largely a compendium of responses to the publication of her autobiography, reflecting the widespread recognition Nin finally received after
the first Diary was issued in 1966. Even though Nin was vindicated by
this response, she was nettled by the critical disapproval or disinterest
which continued in some quarters. As if to drown out the negative voices
afloat in the media, Nin inundates her readers with adulatory messages
which, instead of winning our sympathy, tend to alienate us with their
blatant narcissism. How many times can we read variations on this
theme—"Anais, I read your diaries with speechless admiration."

Nin's defensiveness on the subject of her narcissism takes its most
strident form in this volume. She tells us she is tired of the platitudes
hurled at her: "There was no ego in the Diary, there was only a voice
which spoke for thousands. . . . The two most misinterpreted words in
the world: narcissism and ego. The simple truth was that some of us
recognized the need to develop, grow, expand—occupations which are
the opposite of these two words. To desire to grow means you are not
satisfied with the self as it is, and the ego is exacting, not indulgent"
(200). In the very next paragraph, Nin proceeds to quote testimonials to
her uniqueness which go on for five pages. "You speak rain words which
fill the saucer eye of a parched insomniac"—and more of the same. While
it would be uncharitable not to excuse Nin at least in part on the grounds
of illness and age, the self-justification and self-display apparent here are
also present throughout the Diary. Surely Nin must have realized that
there is no necessary contradiction between narcissism, which has been
defined as "the condition of a subject who prefers never to get out of
himself, even when he appears to do so,"[17] and preoccupation with
growth, as Christopher Lasch argues in his book *The Culture of Narcissism:*
"In order to polish and perfect the part he has devised for himself, the new
Narcissus gazes at his own reflection, not so much in admiration as in
unremitting search of flaws, signs of fatigue, decay."[18] Narcissism has
become, according to many social commentators, one of the primary

themes of our culture, and Nin's Diary reflects this orientation, perhaps accounting in part for its popularity.

Nin's literary reputation will not be helped by this seventh volume, by entries such as the following from 1973, in which she complains about all the people sitting at home watching the Watergate hearings on television, "nourishing themselves on garbage," as she puts it. "I find history repellent, not worthy of attention," she declares. "It is an escape from the real tasks" which she considers to be self-transformation. She then proceeds in the following paragraph to launch into a lengthy assessment of her appearance which must rank as the most unfortunate juxtaposition of two paragraphs in the entire Diary:

Nature was kind to me. First of all, sensual love can continue as long as emotional love is alive. In my case my body was never distorted. My feet are unchanged—the ankles not swollen. I have no varicose veins. I have kept my weight at 120 pounds . . . I have no frown lines between the eyes. I have wrinkles around my eyes, laugh wrinkles, but no pouches. . . . The flesh under my forearm is a little loose. But my breasts are like a young girl's, the nipples pink . . . . I still arouse desire and receive love letters. (276)

The mirror of Nin's last Diary reveals a woman still preoccupied with appearances, as she had been at seventeen, still anxious to arouse desire as a confirmation of her value. She remains, to the end, transfixed by her looking-glass image, waiting to receive the ultimate approval never forthcoming. Surrounded by adulatory letters, like her father's photographs of himself, she is still, in the end, unsure.

Chapter Four

House of Incest:
Through a Glass Darkly

Through the Looking Glass

House of Incest, Nin's first published work of fiction (1936), is another version of *Through the Looking Glass* with Alice transformed to Anaïs but disguised as an unnamed narrator who takes us on a tour of her inner nightmares. This surrealist prose poem, a haunting excursion into a woman's private realm, is the most effective piece of writing outside the Diary Nin composed. Despite the overabundance of imagery at times, and the amorphous structure of the piece, *House of Incest* contains some of the most compelling passages in all Nin's work. In descending into her inferno and making art out of its dangerous depths, Nin was able to transcend the limitations of life lived before the mirror, and to move out toward the world denied the inhabitants of *House of Incest.* For her *House* consists of a medley of voices which reflect not only the particular anguish of the writer's dreams and existence, but the experience of innumerable women past if not present: voices of isolation and fragmentation, enclosure and self-division.

In keeping with the traditional framework of woman's existence, *House* is a completely hermetic work: air-tight, claustrophobic in the extreme. Virtually all the action takes place within the woman's realm: the house. The outer world, when it appears at all, is seen "through a glass darkly." The windows in this house "gave out on a static sea, where immobile fishes had been glued to painted backgrounds" (51–52). Communication between the people in this house takes place through "little spying-eyed windows," and sounds of the "street organ and the apple vendor" come muffled through a shell. The chief source of entrapment here is narcissism, self-obsession: "If only we could all escape from this house of incest, where we only love ourselves in the other. . ." (70). This psychological motif informs the entire prose poem, and as we have already seen, much of Nin's writing.

"It is the seed of all my work," Nin said about *House,* "the poem from which the novels were born."[2] Not only is "seed" appropriate because *House* embodies in nascent form Nin's lifetime themes and concerns, but also because this is a book about birth—about the birth of the woman artist and the creation of her first work of art, which are of course inseparable. Otto Rank, who had such a great influence on Nin, particularly during the years of composition of this work, said the first creative act of the artist is the re-creation of his (her) personality. *House* is a mythic tale of the struggle toward re-creation of the woman artist's personality which necessarily takes place not only in, but through, the looking glass.

In their book, *The Madwoman in the Attic,* Gilbert and Gubar treat the looking glass as one of the central metaphors for the woman writer's efforts at self-definition. They quote from Mary Coleridge's poem, "The Other Side of the Mirror," which in many ways duplicates Nin's own peculiar tale.[3] As Mary Coleridge sat before her glass one day and "conjured up a vision bare. . . . The vision of a woman, wild / With more than womanly despair," so did Nin's first creative act of self-contemplation in the mirror of her book also yield a vision of "womanly despair," made more frightening by the recognition of her own "shadow in the glass." She too felt that she "had no voice to speak her dread," partly no doubt because the literary tradition behind her was so overwhelmingly male. But in conjuring up her "vision bare," Nin found that she was speaking with "more than womanly despair," echoing the voices of the stifled generations of women behind her, reflecting their "speechless woe."

A Woman's *Season in Hell*

Nin referred to her book several times as a "woman's *Season in Hell,*" alluding not only to the fact that this is a woman's version of a descent into the self, but also to the influence of Rimbaud, whose book of that name served her as a model in her undertaking. It was Rimbaud's excursion into the unconscious, his *Season in Hell,* which encouraged Nin to embark on her own nightmare voyage. Both works participate in the ancient tradition of a "descent into the inferno" which is the self, a journey invariably fraught with dangers, since it exposes the participant to deeply repressed fears and desires, to the forces of personal disintegration. However, the rewards of this dangerous undertaking potentially outweigh the costs, as the prospect at journey's end is for a sense of reintegration and wholeness, and for the artist in particular, a world of imaginative richness perhaps unavailable otherwise. In his famous "Lettre du Voyant" written in 1871, Rimbaud spoke of the artist's task as a "long, immense and reasoned *deranging* of *all his senses*" as a means of reaching a transcendent state, which he calls the "unknown."[4] He recommends experiencing all forms of love, suffering, madness, exhausting oneself in all their poisons, in order to preserve their essence. *House of Incest* is Nin's response to Rimbaud's advice.

For Nin, Rimbaud was a "liberating force," giving her the courage to "break with realism." The surrealists, including André Breton, who were also powerfully influenced by Rimbaud, supported this inclination. Their emphasis on an antirealist and anticonformist attitude toward art clearly effected Nin. Her description of what the inferno means to her sounds like a surrealist program: "My descent into the inferno is a descent into the irrational level of existence, where the instincts and blind emotions are loose, where one lives by pure impulse, pure fantasy, and therefore pure madness" (I, 36). Breton's advocacy of free association and automatic writing as a means of tapping the rich imagery of the unconscious was particularly germane to Nin, as this passage from Diary I suggests: "I have always believed in André Breton's freedom, to write . . . in the order and disorder in which one feels and thinks, to follow sensations and absurd correlations of events and images. . ." (11). J. H. Matthews's description of a surrealist novel as a "hallucinatory succession of contradictory images superimposed, one upon the other,"[5] is a perfect summary of *House,* although Nin's prose poem diverges from "pure" surrealist aims in that she does not exhibit the usual "mistrust for psychological penetration" so much as an equivocal attitude toward its virtues.

To Proceed from the Dream Outward

It was C. G. Jung's phrase—"To proceed from the dream outward"—which Nin says fired her to begin writing *House.* She kept a record of her dreams for a year and used them as the basis for her prose poem. In Diary I she mentions that she began the first two pages of *House* in 1932 a few days after undertaking psychoanalysis with Dr. René Allendy, suggesting that the process of analysis—of free association and emphasis on dreams—stimulated and supported her in this endeavor.

During the course of her analysis and association with Dr. Otto Rank the shape of *House* emerged.[6] In Diary II, Nin verifies Rank's role in helping her to perceive the design of her first work and to finish *House* (31). His books on the trauma of birth, the theme of the double, and neurosis and art struck a respondent chord in Nin, serving as a confirmation of her own themes. Perhaps most important was Rank's encouragement of Nin's effort to reconstruct herself in legendary fashion. *House* is Nin's first creative venture in this process of reconstruction.

Miller and Nin: Dynamic Duo

Henry Miller also played a decisive role in the composition of *House*. Not only did he edit versions of *House* Nin produced during the three years she worked on the manuscript, but he also suggested the title (unacknowledged by Nin), since his first novel, written in his head as a young man, was "The House of Incest."[7] In addition, *House* was to some extent the product of a collaboration between Nin and Miller on a film script. When they first met, a mutual enthusiasm for surrealist film sparked ideas in both. Miller wrote in the margins of Nin's "House" manuscript, "All pictorial passages wonderful. Would make a film script" (I, 266). They began to compose a scenario together, each taking turns writing a scene. "We enlarge, probe my sketchy material," Nin explained in Diary I. In recalling this collaboration at a later date, Nin claimed she disbanded the idea of them working together when she realized their styles "could not fuse." "I quietly left out of my final version the themes Henry had developed in his own way and in his own language. Henry felt he had been stimulated by *House of Incest* material and insisted on saying it was inspired by it" (II, 245).

Apparently they were both stimulated by this undertaking, though it is impossible at this point to be certain who was responsible for what images or scenes worked out together. Miller's end of the collaboration led to "Scenario" which was published by Obelisk Press, read over the French radio, and recorded. Nin's *House of Incest* was published by Siana Editions (Anaïs spelt backward), another joint venture, in 1936, in a very limited edition, reissued by Nin's Gemor Press in 1947 and again, in 1958 by Swallow Press with the inclusion of photomontages by Val Telberg, but it has never reached the audience that Miller's "Scenario" has.

Discussions between Nin and Miller on dreams also helped to generate the text of *House*. Nin records her assertion to Miller in Diary I that "most dreamwriting is false and intellectually composed," the same quarrel she had with the surrealists and Joyce. After reading Miller's dream writing in 1934 she comments, "It all needed to be blurred, the outline must be less definite, one image must run into another like water colors" (I, 306). She suggests there must be a "condensation of words" and an absence of "logical, conscious explanation." These interchanges on dream writing apparently helped Nin to clarify the direction she wished to go in her own dream book, which has all the characteristics she notes above.

Perhaps most fruitful in the exchanges between Nin and Miller were the dialogues on the subject of their mutual obsession: Henry's wife June (see Chapter 3). Nin was challenged to take her inclination for the myth, the legendary aspects of June's personality, to the furthest limit by virtue of their joint literary efforts on the same subject. Nin's expansion of June's character in the first portion of Diary I and the second section of *House* represents her writing at its most inspired.

An Edifice without Dimension

"All that I know is contained in this book written without witness," Nin announces in the epigraph to *House*, "an edifice without dimension, a city hanging in the sky." *House* is indeed an "edifice without dimension"—without external form. It is structured loosely as a series of seven surrealist fragments, "visionary symbolic dream sequences," as Nin describes them. Each segment may be regarded as a meditation in which dream images are woven together around certain themes. Although this "edifice" lacks a traditional structure, it is held together by the narrator's perspective, the unnamed "I" who weaves these images and moves throughout the seven sequences. Her place of habitation is both below and above ordinary reality, a "city hanging in the sky"— autonomous, self-contained, remote.

In the second prologue, Nin switches from an abstract to a more visceral dimension: "The morning I got up to begin this book I coughed. Something was coming out of my throat: it was strangling me. I broke the thread which held it and yanked it out. I went back to bed and said: I have just spat out my heart." In concentrated form, Nin alludes here to the painful, compulsive aspect of the creative process. The deeply personal nature of her material is also made clear: it is her heart which must be exposed and relinquished in expelling the book. There is pain and yet liberation in the activity, since the artist, in breaking the cord and releasing the book, yanks both the book and herself into new life.

Nin recites the legend of the Indian who made a flute out of the bones of his dead mistress whom he worshipped. This flute had a "more penetrating, more haunting sound than the ordinary flute. Only I do not wait for my love to die." Not only does the writer's own heart get incorporated into her art, but also the marrow of those she loves. There is a cannibalistic aspect to the creative process; the writer is a giant maw, devouring those whom she worships.

Part One: Submergence

In the first of the seven dream fragments, we are submerged in an aqueous environment as if in preparation for this nightmare voyage. The first-person narrator speaks in an incantatory tone, lulling us (and herself) into a state of receptivity to the unconscious. Photomontages by Val Telberg opposite the first page, and interspersed throughout the book, contribute to the somnolent, hypnotic atmosphere. The narrator cuts the "air with wide-slicing fins, and swim[s] through wall-less rooms." Her bones move "as if made of rubber." She sways and floats, "listening for distant sounds." There were "no currents of thought" in this *House,* "only the caress of flow and desire mingling."

Nin strives to suggest both the blissful state before birth ("I remember my first birth in water"), as well as the prospect of rebirth: "I looked with chameleon eyes upon the changing face of the world, looked with anonymous vision upon my uncompleted self" (15). She evokes this in-between state in which the narrator is haunted by "lost sounds" and "lost colors," "standing forever on the threshold like one troubled with memories." Both the earliest memories of childhood and the as-yet-undiscovered self of the future are associated with Atlantide—Nin's version of Atlantis, the legendary sunken island.[8] Through the "route of the dream" the narrator suggests the possibility of uncovering this rich unknown. But the remainder of part one dwells almost exclusively on the pleasures of submergence rather than recovery: "I loved the ease and the blindness and the suave voyages on the water bearing one through obstacles. The water was there to bear one like a giant bosom" (16).

The seductive ease and tranquillity of this dream state punctuated by the sound of the "bells of Atlantide" cannot last indefinitely. It ends with a sudden jolt into the harsh realities of the day: "I awoke at dawn, thrown up on a rock, the skeleton of a ship choked in its own sails" (17). This last image serves as a powerful reminder of the dangers of this descent into the self, into the "voicelessness of the dream"—namely of self-consumption. It is a presage of what lies ahead and a forewarning to readers inclined to embark on their own inner voyages.

Part Two: Two Profiles of the Same Soul

The second section of *House* has a haunting power and dramatic intensity which make it outstanding in this work. Here Nin expands upon the myth of June Miller as Sabina, first introduced in Diary I. This myth includes the universal drama of the double, made famous by works such as Dostoevsky's *The Double,* Conrad's *Secret Sharer,* and Poe's "William Wilson." As in the classic double tale, Nin's variation on the Doppelgänger involves a mysterious identification and projection between two members of the same sex which seems both real and unreal. There is a psychological authenticity to this drama in all these cases which gives it an almost superreality, yet the distinctions between personalities, between dream and reality, are so indistinct as to lend an aura of unreality to the double tale. It is impossible to be certain in this genre whether one is dealing with two separate individuals or a split within one; they are both plausible explanations. Hence this sequence can be read as a drama involving the narrator, who is a writer, and Sabina, the *femme fatale* who captivates her; in this case, the writer is fascinated by a woman who represents her mirror-opposite, her double or shadow—all that she fantasizes she could be or fears she is. At the same time, this is a psychological tale dealing with the narrator's surface personality, her persona or mask, and her shadow self, the darker side of her nature she usually keeps hidden from view. From either viewpoint, the exploration of this mirror-opposite can be both a fascinating and frightening undertaking.

From the opening paragraph, it is clear the narrator has been thrown off-kilter, become "unglued" by her fascination for her double. "The day and night unglued, and I falling in between not knowing on which layer I was resting, whether it was the cold grey upper leaf of dawn, or the dark layer of night" (18). Sabina is the cause of this disruption, the dark lady of the night, whose face first appears "suspended in the darkness of the garden," a "luminous mask . . . waxy, immobile, with eyes like sentinels." She is larger than life, primeval in her associations: "She stared with such an ancient stare, heavy luxuriant centuries flickering in deep processions." The basis for her power, as with the age-old female stereotype, is her irresistible sensuality: "Every gesture she made quickened the rhythm of the blood and aroused a beat chant like the beat of the heart of the desert, a chant which was the sound of her feet treading down into the blood the imprint of her face." Appropriate to her role as a shadow figure, there is an anti-social element to her nature, a distinct streak of cruelty, with her "necklace thrown around the world's neck, unmeltable.

She carried it like a trophy wrung of groaning machinery, to match the inhuman rhythm of her march" (21).

The narrator is blinded by her infatuation for her mirror-opposite: "her breath on my vision like human breath blinding a mirror." She feels shattered by her double, by the prospect of endless self-duplication: "One woman within another eternally, in a far-reaching procession, shattering my mind into fragments, into quarter tones which no orchestral baton can ever make whole again" (22). Despite the sense of fragmentation, the narrator exults in their mutual recognition: "And she and I, we recognized each other; I her face and she my legend." The distinctions between them become blurred: "Deep into each other we turned our harlot eyes. She was an idol in Byzance, an idol dancing with legs parted; and I wrote with pollen and honey. The soft secret yielding of woman I carved into men's brains with copper words; her image I tattooed in their eyes. They were consumed by the fever of their entrails, the indissoluble poison of legends. If the torrent failed to engulf them, or did they extricate themselves, I haunted their memory with the tale they wished to forget." Sabina's desire to tread "down into the blood the imprint of her face" is duplicated in the writer's determination to "carve" into men's brains her image and the "soft secret yielding of woman." Nin's childhood ambition to use her pen as her sword surfaces in this frightening image of determination to conquer men with her erotic literary brew. They both turn into sirens of old, of whom men must beware.

The writer's mask of normality has been disrupted by her total identification with her mirror-opposite. She attempts to reclaim her original role as integrator and "keeper of fragile things," perhaps in response to this disruption. "I was carrying her fetiches, her marionettes, her fortune teller's cards worn at the corners like the edge of a wave" (24). She plays mother and caretaker, instead of spellbound mirror; a hint of disillusionment sets in: "The windows of the city were stained and splintered with rainlight and the blood she drew from me with each lie, each deception." But rather than come to grips with Sabina's deception, she contrives a defensive explanation reminiscent of Nin's justification in her Diary for her need of illusion:

Your lies are not lies, Sabina. They are arrows flung out of your orbit by the strength of your fantasy. To nourish illusion. To destroy reality. I will help you: it is I who will invent lies for you and with them we will traverse the world. But behind our lies I am dropping Ariadne's golden thread—for the greatest of all joys is to be able to retrace one's lies, to return to the source and sleep one night a year washed of all superstructures. (26)

The same image of Ariadne's golden thread recurs in the Diary—Nin's means of retracing her steps to the past—but in both instances it becomes increasingly difficult despite this thread to feel "washed of all superstructures."

Meanwhile, the writer is in danger of drowning like Narcissus in her reflective pool: "Your beauty drowns me, drowns the core of me. When your beauty burns me I dissolve as I never dissolved before man. From all men I was different, and myself, but I see in you that part of me which is you. I feel you in me; I feel my own voice becoming heavier, as if I were drinking you in, every delicate thread of resemblance being soldered by fire and one no longer detects the fissure." This last image bears a striking resemblance to the central image in Bergman's film *Persona*, also a drama of identification and mergence between two women (or two sides of one) played out until their two faces merge on the screen.[9] Nin comments on the resemblance in later years and adds, "Sabina and the writer of the poem are in constant danger of identifying with each other and *becoming the other*" (NF, 122–23).

Just before the two identities merge completely, the writer pauses to consider her own invisibility, clearly a situation she hopes to alter through becoming this other, more visible personage: "Sabina, you made your impression upon the world. I passed through it like a ghost. Does anyone notice the owl in the tree at night, the bat which strikes the window pane while others are talking, the eyes which reflect like water and drink like blotting paper." Finally, this question is capitalized on the page: "DOES ANYONE KNOW WHO I AM?"—which of course is the issue behind the construction of this tale. Through Sabina, and through writing the book, the narrator-writer hopes to make herself known to herself and to the world, to release herself from confinement and embalmment: "I was embalmed in my own secret vertigoes."

Finally this interrelated desire to be known and be one with Sabina reaches its culmination in a remarkable image of identity interchange and fusion—an exact verbal counterpart to Bergman's screen variation on this theme. "So now we are inextricably woven. . . . Our faces are soldered together by soft hair, soldered together, showing two profiles of the same soul" (28). In the film, the faces of the two women are literally merged into a single face, at first obviously off-kilter, then disturbingly integrated. It is an indelible image in both forms of integration and self-division at once, a picture of unity between mask and shadow, between two women, and of eternal division. The emotional intensity of this scene is accentuated by the inclusion of the audience in this extraordinary moment. The following words appear centered on the page:

I AM THE OTHER FACE OF YOU . . .
THIS IS THE BOOK YOU WROTE
AND YOU ARE THE WOMAN
I AM

Through this enlargement of the words, the reader is brought into the drama of identity interchange, encouraged to project into the text and fantasize about unimagined possibilities, creative and otherwise. The enlarged "I AM" also suggests the writer-narrator's achievement of a moment of wholeness, selfhood through this merging with her mirror-opposite, or between her own persona and shadow.

But the moment does not last. Inevitably, it dissolves because of the difficulty of maintaining a sense of wholeness within a fragmented self, between two people, or in a shattered world. The dissolution of the bond also suggests the effects of the homosexual taboo and/or a reluctance or incapacity to confront the submerged self. There is a noticeable disintegration within the narrator immediately afterwards: "I am ill with the obstinacy of images, reflections in cracked mirrors. I am a woman with Siamese cat eyes smiling always behind my gravest words, mocking my own intensity. I smile because I listen to the OTHER and I believe the OTHER. I am a marionette pulled by unskilled fingers, pulled apart, inharmoniously dislocated; one arm dead, the other rhapsodizing in mid-air" (29–30).

As in the Diary, Nin produces her most inspired writing in *House* when she describes the sensation of self-division. The mirror has cracked and the woman is in fragments, "pulled apart, inharmoniously dislocated," like Sylvia Plath's heroine in *The Bell Jar*. Instead of playing the role of caretaker of Sabina's marionettes, she now recognizes herself as the marionette, subject to the caprice and influence of others, unknown to herself. Her sense of self has been "dislocated" by this mergence with her mirror image. She is divided between the reflection of herself which she presents to please the others—in stereotypic female fashion—and the buried shadow which has appeared as a result of this identification. Images of her own perversity appear to her in "cracked mirrors," threatening to catapult her into insanity: "I see two women in me freakishly bound together, like circus twins. I see them tearing away from each other. I can hear the tearing, the anger and love, passion and pity. When the act of dislocation suddenly ceases—or when I cease to be aware of the sound—then the silence is more terrible because there is nothing but insanity around me, the insanity of things pulling, pulling within oneself, the roots tearing at each other to grow separately, the strain made to achieve unity" (30).

There is no distinguishing the "pulling within" and without; the conflict between the two women is duplicated in an interior self-division, the inner insanity is matched by the outer. The writer and Sabina have "leaped beyond cohesion," as has the narrator herself. From this point, the remainder of the sequence demonstrates the dislocation which has occurred. Everything is magnified and distorted, as in a funhouse mirror, yet there is a hallucinatory vividness to the imagery which makes it most effective.

Some of the images depict nightmare scenes of confinement and entrapment so common in women's literature. "The smallness of a room is like that of an iron cage in which one can neither sit nor lie down." Cellars have fires "hissing" in them and attics threaten the narrator with "open scissors." "Attic windows. I lie on a bed like gravel. All connections are breaking. Slowly I part from each being I love, slowly, carefully, completely. . . . I die in a small scissor-arched room, dispossessed of my loves and my belongings, not even registered in the hotel book. At the same time I know that if I stayed in this room a few days an entirely new life could begin—like the soldering of human flesh after an operation" (31–32).

She realizes her emotional pain could heal, but it is "the terror of this new life, more than the terror of dying, which arouses" her. Recovery, however, may be possible through the restorative power of words: "I writhed within my own life, seeking a free avenue to carry the molten cries, to melt the pain into a cauldron of words for everyone to dip into, everyone who sought words for their own pain. What an enormous cauldron I stir now; enormous mouthfuls of acid I feed the others now, words bitter enough to burn all bitterness" (32). Melting the pain into a "cauldron of words" may provide at least temporary relief for the writer and reader, but it is also profoundly disturbing since the writer regards what she is producing as "enormous mouthfuls of acid." This was the danger implicit in this journey from the start—"Disrupt the brown crust of the earth and all the sea will rise." The sea of the unconscious—buried fears and desires—has risen and drowned the writer, dispersing identity, meaning in a chaos of images which nevertheless are potent. "Reality was drowned and fantasies choked each hour of the day" (34).

Part Three: The Fissure in Reality

Part three is the voice of the drowned woman. After "collision with reality," the narrator retreats to the dream, falls into darkness, and then makes the "divine departure," her "head pulled up by the clouds and swinging in space." She is in terror of her "ascensions," but they are beyond her control: "When human pain has struck me fiercely, when anger has corroded me, I rise, I always rise after the crucifixion, and I am in terror of my ascensions. THE FISSURE IN REALITY" (37). Her words are reminiscent of Sylvia Plath's in "Lady Lazarus": "Beware / Beware. / Out of the ash / I rise with my red hair / And I eat men like air."[10] It is her inevitable separation from ordinary reality which torments the narrator now: "Distance. I never walked over the carpet into the ceremonies. Into the fullness of the crowd life, into the authentic music and the odor of men. I never attended the wedding or the burial. Everything for me took place either in the belfry where I was alone with the deafening sound of bells calling in iron voices, or in the cellar where I nibbled at the candles and the incense stored away with the mice" (38–39). Other images of female madness and confinement come to mind with this passage—Mrs. Rochester's isolation in the attic in Brontë's *Jane Eyre,* the young girl's consignment to the cellar in Marguerite Duras's *Hiroshima Mon Amour.*

What becomes increasingly apparent in this section is the extent of the narrator's paranoia which is, of course, a manifestation of guilt and self-preoccupation. "I am an insane woman for whom houses wink and open their bellies. Significance stares at me from everywhere, like a gigantic underlying ghostliness. . . . Behind windows there are either enemies or worshippers. Never neutrality or passivity. Always intention and premeditation" (39–40). The narrator-writer is trapped in the "poisoned web" of her self-absorption. It is she, not Sabina, who is now caught in her lies: "I am enmeshed in my lies, and I want absolution. I cannot tell the truth because I have felt the heads of men in my womb. The truth would be death-dealing and I prefer fairytales. I am wrapped in lies which do not penetrate my soul. As if the lies I tell were like costumes . . . the moment I step into the cavern of my lies I drop into darkness. I see a face which stares at me like the glance of a cross-eyed man" (40, see I,

127). Part of the "fissure in reality" comes from this frightening gap between the narrator's lies which she wears like "costumes" and her real self which is impenetrable. This disturbing revelation is the real end point of the third sequence, followed by a passage of planetary purplish prose which undercuts the effectiveness of what came before: "I remember the cold on Jupiter freezing ammonia and out of ammonia crystals came the angels. . . . I remember the tornadoes of inflammable methane on Saturn. I remember on Mars a vegetation like the tussock grasses of Peru and Patagonia, an ochrous red, a rusty ore vegetation, mosses and lichens. Iron bearing red clays and red sandstone. . . ." The narrator-writer ascends through a smokescreen of surreal images when the revelations become too painful.

Parts Four through Six: Inside the House of Incest

In the three sections which follow, Nin introduces the third inhabitant of this *House* aside from the narrator-writer and Sabina (who disappears after part two)—Jeanne, a character who also figures in the Diary. In the first Diary, Nin says about her: "I saw the lightness and the masks, the leaps into space, even into madness, as ways to out-distance the unutterable incest" (169). Jeanne is the voice through which the "unutterable incest" is first expressed, and through her the narrator confronts and exposes her own buried incestuous desires. She is another double for the narrator, and plays out a double drama with her own brother as well.

Jeanne, with her "noble-raced profile," "crippled leg," and "nerve-stained fingers" bears a distinct resemblance to Roderick Usher in that other famous incest tale, Poe's "Fall of the House of Usher,"[11] but she is closer still to the narrator of whom she is another reflection. The theme of narcissism associated indirectly with the narrator becomes explicit in her case: "She picked up a mirror and looked at herself with love. Narcisse gazing at himself in Lanvin mirrors" (44). Later she sits before her mirror once again and wonders how all her "separate pieces" can add up to a whole person: "When I sit before my mirror I laugh at myself. I am brushing my hair. Here are a pair of eyes, two long braids, two feet. I look at them like dice in a box, wondering if I should shake them, would they still come out and be ME. I cannot tell how all these separate pieces can be ME" (47–48). While her proclamation of love for her brother is writ large—"I LOVE MY BROTHER"—he is clearly as much a figment of her imagination as Sabina is of the narrator's: "Our love of each other is like one long shadow kissing, without hope of reality" (48).

Most persuasive in Jeanne's monologue is her description of the nightmare experience which accompanied her marriage: "When I heard the bells ringing I thought they rang far too loud. They deafened me. I felt I would begin to weep blood, my ears hurt me so much. . . . I tried to run away from the bells. I shouted: stop the bells from ringing! But I could not run away from them because the sound was all round me and inside me, like my heart pounding in huge iron beats. . ." (45). She is literally "under a glass bell," an image developed by Nin in a short story of that name, and later by Sylvia Plath in *The Bell Jar.* Marriage for Plath's heroine, as for this resident of the *House of Incest,* means unbearable confinement and implosion. Jeanne fears the isolation she associates with marriage, but equally as much, she is in terror of intimacy, another common characteristic for the inhabitants of this *House:* "I have such a fear of finding another like myself, and such a desire to find one! I am so utterly lonely, but I also have such a fear that my isolation be broken through, and I no longer be the head and ruler of my universe. I am in great terror of your understanding by which you penetrate into my world; and then I stand revealed and I have to share my kingdom with you" (46–47).

The narrator's identification with Jeanne's words is apparent; she intervenes for the first time in this sequence and advises Jeanne: "But Jeanne, fear of madness, only the fear of madness will drive us out of the precincts of our solitude, out of the sacredness of our solitude" (47). Clearly the dangers of life "under a glass bell" outweigh the allurements of this sanctified existence. The narrator concludes with these words which are a warning to all inhabitants of the *House of Incest:* "Worlds self-made and self-nourished are so full of ghosts and monsters."

Jeanne's "self-nourished" love for her brother is not developed in the prose poem. Far more than with Sabina in the second sequence, Jeanne's brother is purely a shadow figure—"I kissed his shadow and this kiss did not touch him, this kiss was lost in the air and melted with the shadow" (48). Jeanne searches through the house of incest for her brother in section six, asking everyone to hang something out of their windows so she can find the room where he is hiding. She discovers one window with the "blind shut tight and rusty, one window without light like a dead eye, choked by the hairy long arm of old ivy" (60). This terrifying image of the deadliness of her obsession, the stultifying effects of self-love, is followed by the painful realization that she loves no one: "I love no one, not even my brother. I love nothing but this absence of pain, this cold neutral absence of pain." Eventually she discovers her brother asleep "among the paintings." "I fell in love with your portrait," he tells her, "because it will never change. I have such a fear of seeing you grow old, Jeanne; I fell in love with an unchanging you that will never be taken away from me" (61). Jeanne's brother, like Dorian Gray in Wilde's novel, is the narcissist who, preoccupied with the painted image of his own youthful perfection (reflected in his sister), stagnates amidst his fascination. The fear of death associated with narcissism is also apparent in this Wilde-inspired scene which ends appropriately: "They bowed to one part of themselves only—their likeness."

It is Jeanne who leads the writer in the fifth section into the house of incest itself. In a scene reminiscent of Fellini's *Juliet of the Spirits,* the narrator describes the rooms as "chained together by steps" with no room on a level with another. People communicate through "little spying-eyed windows" between the rooms which are filled with the sound of the sea coming from sea shells. The windows look out on a static sea "where immobile fishes had been glued to painted backgrounds." Because all the inhabitants are imprisoned by self-absorption, no one moves in this house: "they all had such a fear of movement and warmth, such a fear that all love and all life should flow out of reach and be lost!" (52).

Finally, in a scene which has its counterpart in the opening situation in Diary I, the writer describes the room "which could not be found, a room without [a] window, the fortress of their love." In Diary I, Nin describes her house in Louveciennes with its extra shutter put there for symmetry only; she says she often dreams about this "mysterious room which does not exist behind the closed shutter." The mysterious room metamorphoses in her dream book into the setting for the "unutterable incest," the imagined union between daughter and father. This love is not dramatized, only hinted at through a series of suggestive images: "The collision between their resemblances, shedding the odor of tamarisk and sand, of rotted shells and dying sea-weeds, their love like the ink of squids, a banquet of poisons." The narrator seems to try to escape at first from the manifestation of her frightening desires. She stumbles from room to room, only to find herself confronted with a painting of "Lot with his hand upon his daughter's breast while the city burned behind them"—the same painting which fascinated Nin on a museum excursion with Artaud in Diary I. What Nin emphasizes here is not the writer's fear but her joy at this image: "Joy of the father's hand upon the daughter's breast, the joy of the fear racking her" (55). Incest seems to be more horrifying to others than to the father and daughter in this case: "No cry of horror from Lot and his daughter but from the city in flames. . ." (55).

After this admission, albeit abstract, of the "unutterable," there is a subsequent disintegration into a plethora of images, as before. The most striking series is of a "forest of decapitated trees, women carved out of bamboo, flesh slatted like that of slaves in joyless slavery, faces cut in two by the sculptor's knife, showing two sides forever separate, eternally two-faced, and it was I who had to shift about to behold the entire woman" (55). Embedded in these images is the suggestion that women are forever self-divided, this woman in particular because beneath her mask she has followed too many shadow fantasies and desires. It is only through her art that the writer has the possibility of wholeness, of shifting about "to behold the entire woman." Yet she laughs at the pretensions of art, even while maintaining hope in its efficacy: "Further a forest of white plaster, white plaster eggs. Large white eggs on silver disks, an elegy to birth, each egg a promise, each half-shaped nascence of man or woman or animal not yet precise. Womb and seed and egg, the moist beginning being worshipped rather than its flowering. The eggs so white, so still, gave birth to hope without breaking, but the cut-down tree lying there produced a green live branch that laughed at the sculptor" (56). Nin's vision of "womb and seed and egg," inspired by Brancusi's sculpture, expresses a note of optimism about the human potential for growth, despite what appears to be eternal self-division.

Part Seven: Dancing toward Daylight

The narrator-writer turns to her "own book, seeking peace," in the seventh section, but instead she "bruises" herself against her madness. The "reflections in cracked mirrors" which fill this *House* are jagged reminders of dreams and desires perhaps best forgotten: "As I move within my book I am cut by pointed glass and broken bottles in which there is still the odor of sperm and perfume" (62). "What is it allotted me to say?" she wonders. "Only the truth disguised in a fairytale, and this is the fairytale behind which all the truths are staring as behind grilled mosque windows" (67). But the falsity of her "fairytale" apparently disturbs her, leading her to magnify on the page: "LIES CREATE SOLITUDE." Immediately afterward, however, she walks away from this revelation "into the paralytic's room."

The paralytic, like the other residents introduced in this final section, is an artist and also a double of the narrator-writer. He is more consoling in his sameness than disturbing, dealing with issues which can be considered from a position of relative equanimity. "I swallow my own words," he says, "I chew and chew everything until it deteriorates," making him an embodiment of the self-consumptive artist described in the prologue. This blocked artist suffers, as Nin does in the Diary, from his awareness of the limitations of art over life: "I want to tell the whole truth, but I cannot tell the whole truth because I would have to write four pages at once, like four long columns simultaneously, four pages to the present one, and so I do not write at all." Anna, the woman writer in Doris Lessing's *Golden Notebook,* has the identical perspective which leads to her keeping four separate notebooks, but she too is painfully aware of the disparity between the compexity of her experience and the limitations of fictional form.

We are next introduced to the "modern Christ" modeled after Antonin Artaud, the surrealist iconoclast who, according to Breton, actually went through the mirror.[12] The narrator emphasizes her bond with this figure, saying, "The language of nerves which we both use makes us brothers in writing" (68). The modern Christ then goes on to describe a terrifying dream in which he "stood naked in a garden" without his skin which had been "all gently pulled off." This dream of acute exposure, vulnerability to the outer world ends with his cry, "Do you know what it is to be touched by a human being!"—linking him with Jeanne who also felt threatened by the prospect of physical intimacy.

"If only we could all escape from this house of incest," the modern Christ declares, "where we only love ourselves in the other, if only I could save you all from youselves" (70). Clearly the writer identifies her journey in this book with the modern Christ's mission to save the inhabitants from their neuroses, the same mission Nin proclaims in the Diary. But in both cases, the savior is not distinguishable from the entrapped: "none of us could bear to pass through the tunnel which led from the house into the world on the other side of the walls."

However, the prose poem does conclude on a promising note. The figure of a dancer appears, standing at the center of the room and "dancing the dance of the woman without arms." This woman does not hear what is going on around her, making her an appropriate inhabitant of this house; she dances, laughs, and sings at first "all for herself." But she begins to sing of her dilemma, and in so doing, she enacts a ritual of hope for everyone. She becomes the true artist as savior, even if the first "modern Christ" disappointed in that function. "My arms were taken away from me, she sang. I was punished for clinging. . . . I clutched at the lovely moments of life; my hands closed upon every full hour" (71). The dancer realizes her wish to capture the moment can never be achieved, anymore than can Nin's effort in the Diary to recover the lost sounds and colors of the past, and she relents. She opens her arms "like Christ" in a "gesture of abandon and giving . . . opening her arms and her hands, permitting all things to flow away and beyond her." Her gesture signifies a symbolic acceptance for all the inhabitants of the reality of death and separation (for Nin of the impossibility of capturing the moment), resolving the narcissistic dilemma in abstract form.

"And she danced; she danced with the music and with the rhythm of earth's circles; she turned with the earth turning, like a disk, turning all faces to light and to darkness evenly, dancing towards daylight" (72). At least the possibility of moving from the dark enclosure of the *House of Incest* to the world outside the self is now available. The finale also suggests acceptance of the dark and light sides of the self, of mask and shadow. But there is no clear resolution; the writer ends the book, as she began, moving toward completion of her "uncompleted self," "dancing towards daylight."

Chapter Five

Winter of Artifice: Portrait in a Three-Way Mirror

Variations on a Theme

Winter of Artifice is composed of three variations on the double theme already introduced in *House of Incest*. Since it was begun during the same period in which *House* was composed, it is hardly surprising that it shares themes and images with that book. Each of the three novelettes included in the final edition[1]—"Stella," "Winter of Artifice," and "The Voice"—can be considered one facet of the writer's self-contemplation in a three-way mirror. Much as Nin began her self-definition as a young writer before the glass ("I am writing in front of my three mirrors—and after every other word I look at myself with surprise. . ."), so she continues her fictional elaboration on the quest for identity through the looking glass. No matter where Nin begins—whether it is with the actress Stella alienated from her screen self, the daughter in "Winter" haunted by resemblances to her father, or the patients in the Hotel Chaotica enchanted by the healing powers of the Voice—all her characters turn into doubles of the self familiar to us from the Diary.

While this same self-reflective quality characterized *House,* in that case there was a hallucinatory intensity to the language, along with a highly condensed, poetic format which worked to produce a truly original, effective work of art. However, in *Winter* the style lacks distinction for the most part, and the fragmentary structure is not warranted by a surreal context as it is in *House*. Even in the area of characterization, which one might suppose would be Nin's strength, there are problems. This is partly confirmed by Nin in a passage in Diary III: "If only I could invent, invent other characters. Objective work which would not involve guilt. Rank said woman could not invent. . . . When I started out with an invented character, based always on someone I knew, and then sought to expand, I found myself inside restricted forms. . . . I felt in a tight mold, and returned to my experience which I tried to transpose into other women" (260–61). This seems to be exactly what happened with "Stella," the first piece in *Winter* in the final edition. The "invented character" in this instance, Stella, is patterned after the actress Luise Rainer from Diary III. In the first half of the piece, there are definite correlations with Nin's own themes, but there is a degree of detachment and artistic control which contributes to the effectiveness of this portion of the novelette. Approximately halfway through the tale, however, Nin appears to lose sight of Stella as a character, and to return to her own familiar scenario. "Stella" loses vitality as Nin turns once again to her own face in the glass.

"Stella"

"Stella" is the most successful of the three pieces in this volume, despite its flaws. This is particularly true for the first section which has an emotional intensity and concentrated style akin to *House of Incest*. "Stella" is an autobiographical parable about the woman artist divided between her public persona and her private needs. In Diary III Nin describes the conflict as she sees it in Stella's original, Luise Rainer, and in a fashion also clearly related to her own experience as it is depicted in the Diary:

I see a conflict between the woman and the actress. She wants to act out projections of her self, to be herself on stage, and not become other women. . . . On the other hand, she repudiates the actress which brings an enhanced, heightened vision of life and character. . . . It is a quest for her personal integration rather than the quest of an actress. As if acting would free her of her confused and uncertain self, help her find her core through the roles. . . . The acting is simultaneously a dramatization of a divided self, and at the same time she seeks through it the magic unification, two women made one through a role. (138, 145)

Nin in her Diary and fiction and Stella in her stage performances seek authentic roles (characterizations) which will express aspects of their personalities. But they are unsettled by the illusory nature of the images they project, being all too aware of the enhancement, the idealization brought to these images. Stella watches her "double" on the screen and does not recognize her. She repudiates this image which "was a work of artifice, of lighting, of stage setting." "The woman on the screen went continually forward, carried by her story, led by the plot loaned to her. But Stella, Stella herself was blocked over and over again by inner obstacles" (9). They are both more concerned with resolving their dualities and uncertainties than with working on the craft of their performances: "It is a quest for personal integration rather than the quest of an actress." The hope in both cases is that their artistic projections will lead to a "magic unification, two women made one through the role."

Especially problematic for Nin's character, Stella, is the fact that it is this illusory image to which people respond and fall in love: "They courted the face on the screen, the face of translucence, the face of wax on which men found it possible to imprint the image of their fantasy" (9). Such is the case with Bruno who, like others before him, has fallen in love not with the "real" Stella but the "dream of Stella." Her heightened image at a party captures his attention, and it is almost exclusively this aspect of her personality she continues to show him during their periodic moments of intimacy. Stella is blocked in her enjoyment of this relationship because she is constantly imagining abandonment and betrayal in the smallest incidents and separations, being a victim of the "demon of doubt." "The doubt and fear . . . made her stand apart like some unbending god of ancient rituals watching for this accumulation of proofs, the faithful offering food, blood and their very lives. And still the doubt was there for these were but external proofs and they proved nothing" (24).

Stella withdraws from her involvement with Bruno who cannot satisfy her with adequate proofs of his devotion. She retreats to her "movie star apartment" with its "small turning stairway" graced by a "tall window of square glass bricks. These shone like a quartz cave at night. It was the prism which threw her vision back into seclusion again, into the wall of the self" (25). From this point to the conclusion of the novella, there is an increased fragmentation and over-abstraction to the text. Nin diverts us with a vague description of a film about the Atlantis story which concludes with an "unexpected and terrifying explosion" out of which a "very old, forgotten region" emerges, the buried memories of Stella's unhappy childhood, which bear a striking resemblance to Nin's own childhood recollections, as they are recorded in the Diary.

Stella dissolves and Nin's Diary self-portrait is reformed. "The first mirror had a frame of white wood," she tells us in "Stella" as in the Diary, but instead of there being no Anaïs in the mirror, there is no Stella. She is an actress in both cases, "playing all the parts of characters in French history." Stella returns to her memories of her father who is also an actor, with a distinct resemblance to Nin's own father. Contemplation of the father's duplicity and artificiality leads to denial of the daughter's connection with such behavior, despite the resultant aesthetic inconsistencies. Whereas shortly before, Stella was described as "misleading and misled"—"All that she says about herself is false"—now she is "always sincere, speaking as she feels." Although both daughter and father are actors by profession, the father is condemned for disguising himself, whereas the daughter is praised for her authenticity: "There are those who disguise themselves, like Stella's father, who disguised himself and acted what he was not. But Stella only wanted to transform and enlarge herself and wanted to act only what she felt she was, or could be" (45–46).

The novella concludes with Stella's involvement with Philip, an evident mirror of her father. After describing his Don Juan plumage, Nin makes the comment, "He bore no resemblance to any other person or moment of her life" (47). Eventually Stella recognizes the resemblance and a cloud descends over the affair. She mulls over the lifelong effects of her father's abandonment of her as a child, attributing to this trauma her withdrawal from intimacy. "Asphyxiation of the feelings" has set in, as it has with the father. "Stella" ends with the actress's mask highlighted on the screen, as at the start of this drama, but in the beginning there was a woman behind the mask, disturbed at the artfulness of her disguise, and by the end she has disappeared. There has been an atrophying of the heart, due to bitterness and betrayal. Her face appears on the screen, "immobile like a mask. It was not Stella. It was the outer shell of Stella" (54). Stylistically as well as thematically a certain "atrophy" sets in after the first vital section of "Stella" concludes.

"Winter of Artifice"

"Winter of Artifice" is Nin's attempt to dramatize one of the major legends of her life-work: her reunion with her father, the aging Don Juan and salon musician, after a twenty-year separation. She tells the same story in Diaries I and II in slightly different form. Otto Rank no doubt encouraged Nin to develop this subject which coincided with his own interest in the father-daughter story. Nin quotes him at length on the classic outline of this motif in Diary I, including this noteworthy aside—"but in the traditional story they recognize each other before incest is committed." Does this mean Nin and her father recognize each other only afterward? Surely this is unlikely, but whether or not incest is committed is the great unanswered question of this novella, provoked by

Nin's suggestive writing. No doubt innumerable readers have turned to "Winter of Artifice" from the Diary account of the father-daughter reunion in the idle hope of getting a clearer picture of this romance, but of course their expectations are doomed to disappointment.

Nin has no interest whatsoever in shedding light on this topic, although she is intent on developing the legend of her reunion with her father. This is more difficult in practice than in theory, however, since the material of this myth is so highly explosive. Nin suggests some of the problems in a shorthand entry in Diary III: "Guilt about exposing the father. Secrets. Need of disguises. Fear of consequences. Great conflict here. Division" (260). Perhaps because of this need for disguises and fear of judgment, Nin switches the narrative from its original format in the first person in the 1939 edition to the more impersonal and less engaging third person in subsequent editions.[2] Nin's autobiographical heroine is nameless, with no appellation aside from "she," as the father is known only as "he." Thus she begins the novella: "She is waiting for him. She was waiting for him for twenty years. He is coming today" (55). Nin sacrifices the livelier style and greater sense of authenticity of the early "Winter" for a stilted text which presumably shields the author from the too blatantly autobiographical first-person voice.

It is one thing to deal with taboo subjects under the protective covering of a highly abstract, hallucinatory dream language, as Nin did successfully in *House,* and quite another to explore these same subjects in the penetrating light of a readily comprehensible style. Nin's tendency was to "crystallize" her expression when fear of the world's judgment impeded her flow. Hence in "Winter," at the very moment when daughter and father seem about to consummate their relationship, Nin reverts to a lengthy dream parable which provides a smokescreen through which the reader cannot perceive clearly. Nin puts this section in italic script as if to create the impression that this is an interior monologue in the daughter's mind, in the mode of Joyce or Woolf, but this does not help improve the quality of language which reveals Nin at her worst: *"Can we live in rhythm, my father? Can we feel in rhythm, my father? Can we think in rhythm, my father? Rhythm—rhythm—rhythm"* (88).

Nin's tendency to cover her heroine with a protective cloak appears to have deepened over the years. Whereas in the earlier edition of "Winter," Nin discusses the similarity between daughter and father in their tendency to escape pain, by 1942 she has dissociated the daughter from this distasteful admission:

1939: I thought that in capturing our likenesses I had found the key to this mystery which was, fundamentally, a supreme desire to escape pain. Either into the planets, or into human affections, or into another love. One love as a refuge from another.³ 1942: His fundamental desire was to escape pain, hers to face all of life. (106)

Similarly, in the 1939 edition it is far clearer that the daughter is as much the Don Juan(a) as her father; she chuckles at the resemblances between them in their games and illusions created to please their lovers. Her jealousy when she becomes convinced her father is lying to her about another woman has a substantiality to it completely lacking in the abstracted, depersonalized later edition. "I knew perfectly well he was telling me a lie," she says in the earlier version, "because the rimmel comes off when one weeps, but not the lipstick, and besides all elegant women have acquired a technique of weeping which has no such fatal effect upon the make-up. I knew this from my own experience. You wept just enough to fill the eyes with tears and no more."³ In the later version, the rimmel is described, but outside a human context.

When the father's mask is drawn, the daughter fades from view, despite the familiarity of the theme to readers of Nin's work. We are told that it was his mask which so terrified the daughter as a young girl, and it is the reality of this mask which she cannot accept as an adult. She imagines a "real face" behind it: "The skin did not match the skin of his wrists. It seemed made of earth and papiêr-mâché, not pure skin. There must have been a little space between it and the real face, a little partition through which the breeze could sing" (67–68). Nin's character persists in hoping the situation is not irremediable: "It was difficult for her to believe, as others did, that the mask tainted the blood, that the colors of the mask could run into the colors of nature and poison it. She could not believe that, like the women who had been painted in gold and died of the poison, the mask and the flesh could melt into each other and bring on infection . . . [she was] oblivious of the deformities which could be produced in the soul by the wearing of a mask" (97–98). Her obliviousness to the negative potentialities of mask-wearing may be related to her identification with her father's impenetrable facade. This same obliviousness coats the novella like a thick film on glass. Nin's image late in the story of the daughter's perception of the father sums the situation up perfectly: "She could not see her father clearly any more. . . . Lost in a cold, white fog of falsity. Images distorted as if they were looking through a glass bowl" (117).

Nin asserts that her heroine comes out of the ether of her illusions at the end and recognizes the artificiality of her drama. "At last she was entering the Chinese theatre of her drama and could see the trappings of the play as well as the play itself, see that the settings were made of the cardboard of illusion. She was passing behind the stage and could stop weeping. The suffering was no longer real. She could see the strings which ruled the scenes, the false storms and the false lightning" (118–19). She realizes the fulfillment of this love of her father may have been necessary to fulfill the legend, but not her life. Hence her suffering is "no longer real," but neither is this declaration of new-found insight, unprepared for in the text.

The novella ends with the daughter "coming out of the ether of the past," the same ether she came out of when she had a stillbirth, we are told. Since there is no explanation for the paternity of the child, the context of the narrative implicates the father. "But Miss Nin did not intend for the reader to reach this conclusion," says Oliver Evans, "and the lack of such a reference which would have cleared up the matter, is, she has conceded, a structural flaw in the story."[5] But it is not simply a matter of a "structural flaw," since this sort of omission is characteristic of Nin's method in "Winter." This ambiguous ending is a fitting conclusion to a flawed novella which substitutes indirection and innuendo for a full rendering of the father-daughter story.

"The Voice"

The third novella in the collection, "The Voice," is also problematic in terms of plot and characterization, but it is an interesting experiment. Here Nin attempts to deal in fictional form with the psychoanalytic experience and with Otto Rank, the analyst with whom Nin underwent psychoanalysis and practiced as a lay analyst from 1933–1935. Although the reader does not emerge with a particularly clear impression of Rank as "the Voice" or the many other characters in this novella, there are some haunting monologues here which elaborate upon the psychological motifs throughout Nin's work.

The several characters in this piece, frequently indistinguishable, are all in analysis with the Voice, who remains nameless because he is a symbol to all and insignificant as a human being. Nin sketches, but does not develop, a conflict between his patients' need to idolize him, regard him as a "modern priest" and "Sphinx" and his desire to release himself from the prison of his role as father and confessor. Lilith, one of the main characters in the piece, falls in love with the Voice but realizes, as the heroine in "Winter" does, that she has fallen for a mirage, another illusory father figure. She claims he is more than a symbol to her, but as soon as he strips himself of his priestly garb she turns against him, bitterly describing him as a "dark-skinned mythological crab," a "hysterical stunted child," and more of the same. "He remained nothing but A VOICE," she concludes, reducing the psychoanalyst and his profession, by implication, to a dubious stature. This is confirmed indirectly by the lengthy, abstract, somewhat mystifying dream fragment which ends "The Voice."

Aside from a recapitulation of many of Nin's key themes and images, Nin develops the motif in her finale of the window looking out on two avenues, as her route *"constantly split in two,"* one the route that Proust took, the *"labyrinth of remembrance,"* and the other, her *"answer,"* the *"dream without memory." "Yet I left behind a web of memory which wove itself inexorably and slowed up my walking and dreaming"* (175). No matter how hard Nin tries to follow the path of oblivion through the dream, the pattern of her life is revealed to her—in her dreams and writing—"like a frayed cloth," as in the tapestry of her Diary. Part of her wishes to follow the "labyrinth of remembrance," to hold onto precious moments, to savor the past, yet her writing and psychoanalysis, both of which take her in that direction, lead to revelations too painful to bear. The *"eternal moments,"* she tells us in the last line, are the rare instances when duality evaporates, self-forgetfulness occurs, life and legend *"dovetail."* This is an ideal not realized, however, by the characters all trapped in their roles in this "Winter of Artifice."

Chapter Six
Under a Glass Bell:
Into the Labyrinth

Bell Background

"If I had to choose one book by which I would like to be remembered," Nin once remarked, "it is this one,"[1] referring to her collection of short stories, *Under a Glass Bell*. Many readers have shared Nin's preference, although this viewpoint is by no means unanimous. Oliver Evans regards *Bell* as "certainly one of her best books and one of the most distinguished short story collections published in this country in the forties."[2] Nin's sometime friend, Edmund Wilson, praised the book when it first appeared from Nin's own Gemor Press in 1944. He declared that some of the short stories were "really beautiful little pieces" written in a blend of "sometimes exquisite poetry with a homely realistic observation," but he thought there were also passages "which may perhaps suffer a little from an hallucinatory vein of writing which the Surrealists have overdone: a mere reeling-out of images."[3] Wilson's favorable review was of immense significance to Nin, representing the first important, positive critical reception her work received in the United States. However, this was tempered by the more frequent response, such as Elizabeth Hardwick's in *Partisan Review,* that the stories were "vague, dreamy and mercilessly pretentious."[4]

A handful of the stories in this volume are certainly among the best pieces of writing Nin composed outside the Diary. The condensed format of the short story was perfectly tailored to Nin's gifts and limitations as a writer. Her problems with structure, apparent in the longer works of fiction, are side-stepped thanks to the brevity of the short-story form. The rich imagery and emotional intensity of *House of Incest* also characterize the best stories in this volume, although there is a noticeable tendency, as Wilson pointed out, toward the "mere reeling-out of images."

Under a Glass Bell is a companion piece to the Diary, as is virtually all the work designated "fiction." These stories cannot properly be appreciated outside the Diary context from which they were extracted. Read in conjunction with the Diary, they appear as poetic variations on a theme, some more effective than others. Read in isolation, as they would have been by readers who came across this volume before the Diary was published, they may well have appeared fragmentary and needlessly obscure. No wonder Elizabeth Hardwick concluded that Nin had a "pathological appetite for mystification."[5] Nin refers to a stillbirth, houseboat, immense diary as if the reader were already privy to her life. Perhaps the stories were meant partly to draw the reader into the legend of Nin's existence, as with "Winter of Artifice."

She also no doubt wished to transform her diary entries into publishable form, and short of printing the diaries, she offers these shards instead. "Through the Streets of My Own Labyrinth" is simply an excerpt from the Diary with some editing. In "Birth," she compresses and cuts the Diary account until the story is "gemlike," as she puts it. But Nin's penchant for compression and abstraction in her writing, even more pronounced in her fiction than her Diary, leads to the mystifying element to which Hardwick refers. Henry Miller's criticism comes to mind; his suggestion that Nin "break through" her "watertight abstractions" and "allow them to flow" is applicable to these stories, some of which are beautiful and intriguing, but often half-finished and peculiarly missing a human context despite their emotional intensity.

"Birth"

Such is the case with "Birth," the final story in this volume and one of the best, despite its brevity. It is based upon the dramatic stillbirth sequence which concludes the first Diary with such force. In both the fictional and Diary versions, we are presented with an elemental account of a woman's struggle with and against the delivery of her stillborn child. In the Diary, however, there is a fullness to the account, despite the missing ingredients (such as the identity of the father), which is absent from the fiction. "Birth" focuses solely on the prolonged, painful delivery of the stillborn child, while the Diary version includes some of the emotions which predated and followed this crucial experience.

Prior to the incident, Nin acknowledges in the Diary her feeling that there is no room in her life for the unborn child, since she has too many people to care for already. "My little one, not born yet," she explains to the unborn child, "you are the future. I would prefer to live with men, in the present. . . . You ought to die in warmth and darkness. You ought to die because in the world there are no real fathers, not in heaven or on earth" (I, 338). Not only does she wish the child to die because it would not fit into her life, but because she does not trust "man the father." Within herself, there is still a child "forever wailing inside, wailing the loss of a father." This unborn child only reminds her of her father's desertion, which she has yet to overcome, and her fear of desertion by man who does not wish to be a father: "For as soon as you will be born, as just as soon as I was born, man the husband, lover, friend, will leave as my father did" (I, 339).

It took a good deal of courage for Nin to make these admissions in the Diary, although they are somewhat mollified by subsequent emphasis on the father's unwillingness to play his part ("Man is a child, afraid of fatherhood"), and on her need to embrace and hold the child within her. "A part of me lay passive," she explains in both versions, "did not want to push out anyone, not even this dead fragment of myself, out in the cold, outside of me. All in me which chose to keep, to lull, to embrace, to love . . . all in me which imprisoned the whole world in its passionate tenderness, this part of me would not thrust out the child, even though it had died in me" (UGB, 96).[6] In the short story, this appears as a tender defect, while in the Diary, it is only one half of an ambiguous situation.

In both instances, the tension of the story comes from the struggle between the part of the woman attempting to hold onto all things, including this "dead fragment" within herself, and the part wishing only to be released from this burden. This "dead fragment" is, in addition to the child (within herself) and her past, Nin's Diary which is her burden and her hope which she cannot as yet surrender to the world. Her Diary and the unborn child are "demons" preventing life—"half-choked" between her legs, "strangling" her, as she says in the Diary. The writer is victim and victimizer, "half-choked" by the embodiment of her past within her and in her book, but also half-choking the unborn child and her Diary, both of whom threaten her existence as a writer. In finally releasing the unborn child, she relinquishes her fear of letting go (and her fear of death ultimately), symbolically freeing herself as woman and artist alike, making a new life possible.

In "Birth," the real demon appears to be the doctor more than the unborn child. As an emblem of the mechanical society Nin abhors, the doctor is characterized as an impersonal meddler who attempts to "interfere with his instruments" while the woman fights to determine her own fate, to "struggle with nature," herself, the child, and the meaning she "put[s] into it all." She attributes malice to the doctor who had originally been "devoted and worshipful," as she says in the Diary, and who now "would like to take a knife" to her for not trying harder to expel the child from her womb. Eventually she wins control over her body, in contemporary feminist-heroic fashion, refusing another painful injection and yielding the child, not through drugs, but through magical rites—drumming on her stomach in circles.

While "Birth" can be interpreted as a powerful story of a woman's struggle to give birth to her own identity, not to be defined or delivered by man, even if part of her dies in the process, it is noteworthy that the Diary version argues against such an explanation. Nin concludes her Diary account with the statement that she was meant to be not the mother of children, but a "man's woman," nature shaping her "body for the love of man, not of child." She is willing to be defined by man at this point, so long as he is an artist rather than a "mechanical" or authoritative man in her eyes. She also states in the Diary that the stillbirth led to a "profound ineluctable communion" with God, granting her "connection with God" from "that moment on." If this was indeed the case, Nin is noticeably reticent on the subject of God for the remainder of the Diary. Rather than ascribe such powers to herself, perhaps Nin was more comfortable imagining a higher being responsible for her rebirth as woman artist. In any case, this story in both forms comes closest to Nin's theories about woman's art, to a simple perfection she rarely achieved in her art.

"Houseboat"

"Houseboat," the first story in the collection, retells the story of the vessel which Nin had discovered in Diary II as her proper setting for life and art. Nin omits the background to the purchase of her houseboat and concentrates on the attributes and lore surrounding her vessel. She makes it clear at once that no ordinary, conventional woman resides on this houseboat, but one who has "refused to follow the procession of the streets." Although the "current of the crowds wanted to sweep me along with it," she declares in the first sentence (attributing motives to the crowd that properly belong to the narrator), she "broke away from it like a fallen piece." "I swerved out and stood at the top of the stairs leading down to the Quays" (11), she explains, marking her separation from and perhaps superiority to the multitudes. She, like the "wrecked mariners of the street current" who live in close proximity to the houseboat, "sought the river which lulled them."

Her houseboat offers her a structure for forgetting, for being "carried, lifted, borne down, without feeling the hard bone of pain in man. . . . No shocks, no violence, no awakening" (12). She is safely removed from the difficulties and particulars of ordinary life: "As soon as I was inside of the houseboat, I no longer knew the name of the river or the city" (13). In this interior haven, she can imagine she is voyaging, undisturbed by the incursion of reality. "Every time I inserted the key in the lock, I felt this snapping of cords, this lifting of anchor, this fever of departure. Once inside the houseboat, all the voyages began." Imaginative departures are facilitated by the comforting fact that this dream boat is "tied at the foot of the stairs." It is ever-in-motion, even while there is no danger of actually setting sail for unknown destinations. This enclosed and private vessel is also ideally situated for the "deepest precipices of desire," a possibility not developed here, but suggested in the Diary and more fully in *Four-Chambered Heart*.

The first interruption to this ideal existence comes in a reference to the "Unknown Woman of the Seine," who had drowned herself in the river several years before and "who was so beautiful that at the Morgue they had taken a plaster cast of her face." This anonymous character hovers over the tale and reappears in the form of another would-be victim whose shrieks and choking impose themselves upon this dream vessel. "I arrived just as the woman who was drowning grasped the anchor's chain." Soon thereafter, the narrator awakens, thinking she too is at the bottom of the Seine, making clear her identification with the drowned woman who has twice appeared. Instead of exploring this nightmare, Nin opts for surreal images which "reel-out" rather than reveal: "In this silence and white communion took place the convolutions of plants turning into flesh, into planets. The towers were pierced by swordfishes, the moon of citron rotated on a sky of lava, the branches had thirsty eyes hanging like berries" (18).

In this more abstract, poeticized version of the houseboat motif, Nin is forced to move the boat from its locale because of the impending arrival of the King of England rather than imminent war, as in Diary II. Despite the order to vacate, the narrator resists leaving her berth, believing an exception will be made for her. Finally she is pulled away by a tugboat in a charming scene in which she runs wildly through her houseboat at last in motion, while the tugboat captain's wife matter-of-factly makes lunch on their more pragmatic vessel. Along the way, they manage to pass all the houses where the writer had lived, offering her a contrast between her former captivity and her new-found sense of freedom and mobility.

Although her "Noah's Ark" is deposited in a "slaughterhouse" in the end, its leaks irreparable, the journey toward that destination has at least released the narrator from her stationary, enclosed existence. She is feeling free, even if the vehicle which made that freedom possible has been retired. This charming piece provides a light accompaniment to the description of "La Bella Aurore" in Diary II.

"The Labyrinth"

In one of her most haunting works, "The Labyrinth," Nin meditates upon the diary-writing process through the metaphor of the labyrinth. For those who read this piece before the Diary was published, its effect must have been far different—ambiguous and mystifying in the way that much of Nin's less persuasive writing can be. But with the Diary in hand, its impact is much stronger. There is an authenticity to this cry of anguish by the author trapped too long in the labyrinth of her life-book:

I was eleven years old when I walked into the labyrinth of my diary. . . . I walked protected by dark green shadows and followed a design I was sure to remember. I wanted to remember in order to be able to return. As I walked, I walked with the desire to see all things twice so as to find my way back into them again. . . . I did not count the turns, the chess moves, the meditated displacements, the obsessional repetitions. The repetitions prevented me from counting the hours and the steps. The obsessions became the infinite. I was lost. I only stopped because of the clock pointing to anguish. An anguish about returning, and about seeing these things but once. (63)

Nin summarizes, in condensed form, the hazards of the autobiographical enterprise: the "anguish about returning and about seeing these things but once." The diarist wants to "see all things twice" in order to hold onto the past, yet the effort is doomed to failure, destined to lead to pain and confusion. "I was walking up a stairway of words," she continues. "The words repeated themselves. I was walking on the word pity pity pity pity pity pity. My step covered the whole word each time, but then I saw I was not walking. . . . The word died. And the anguish came, about the death of this word, about the death of the feeling inside of this word" (64). This is the price Nin has paid for her autobiographical art: the death of the language grown stale by self-absorption, self-pity, and repetition, the death of feeling through over-analysis and posturing too long before the mirror.

Nin turns from this painful revelation to the relief of abstractions, dream talk in which meaning is obscured. We are taken through a "tunnel of darkness" on an "escalator of words": "In front of me was a tunnel of darkness which sucked me violently ahead, while the anguish pulled me backwards. The escalator of words ran swiftly under me, like a river. I was walking on my rebellions, stones exploding under my feet. Following the direction of their heaviest fragment might take me back. Yet all the time I knew that what I would find would be white bleached bones, sand ashes, decomposed smiles, eyes full of holes like cooled lava" (64). These images of decomposition, reminiscent of Yves Tanguy's canvases or T. S. Eliot's "The Hollow Men," are part of the modern landscape of despair. The despair in this case comes partly from the narrator's sense that she is subject to emotions over which she has no control. She is more acted upon than acting—sucked violently ahead, pulled backward without exercising her own will. Her attempt to obliterate her anger by covering it over only leads to an extinction of vital emotions, a desiccation of the heart ("bleached bones," "eyes full of holes").

Her tears of self-pity become part of the geography of her form: "My feet were slipping on accumulated tears like the slippery silt of river banks." She touches "rock-crystal walls," suggesting the hardening of feeling, and "white sponges of secret sorrows," related to over-identification and absorption of others, which Nin describes as her downfall in the Diary. The sensation of being sapped by others is also apparent: "Leaves, skins, flesh had been sucked of their juices, and the juices and sap drunk by the crevices, flowing together through the river bed of stillborn desires" (65). This last phrase evokes not only Nin's stillbirth experience, but the desires which are "stillborn" because not expressible in the Diary or unrelieved in satisfactory love relations, in part because the writer has been trapped too long in her interior cave.

The labyrinthian cave of her Diary is decorated with fragments of human beings, pieces of the writer and others offered to the "appetite of the cave, nailed with humble prayers for protection that the demon might not devour those who passed." These particles of human beings are votive offerings meant to ward off the "demon" of despair or death, but despite these "offerings," the diarist is not free. Instead, she is "pinned to a spider web of fantasies spun during the night, obstinately followed during the day." Her dreamed version of life and personality guides her steps, and hence constricts her progress. Tension and conflict keep her entrapped: "I found myself traversing gangways, moats, gangplanks while still tied to the heaving straining cord of a departing ship." As in "Houseboat," she imagines situations of mobility, risk, while tied to the cord of her ship. The difficulties and confusion involved in following her chosen path are perhaps too much for her. She sinks into a "labyrinth of silence," losing her powers of articulation, retreating to a stuporous state suggestive of a drug torpor: "My lips moved like the sea anemone, with infinite slowness, opening and closing . . . forming nothing but a design in water" (65–66). The writer has come to a complete standstill, partly because of the obsessional nature of her quest. "I was not moving any more with my feet. The cave was no longer an endless route opening before me. It was a wooden, fur-lined crib, swinging" (66). Self-reflective writing can lead to regression and immobility rather than the hoped-for growth in awareness and art.

The story ends, as it began, with the "sound of paper unrolling," with the writer treading the paper streets of her Diary. Her feet touch the "leaves of intricate flowers shriveling," indicating the loss of life force in this endless quest. The "white orifice of the endless cave" opens finally, revealing a "girl eleven years old carrying the diary in a little basket" (67). Nowhere else in her writing does Nin dramatize more effectively the circularity of her literary efforts, the self-consuming and constricting aspects of her labyrinthian Diary.

"Hejda"

"Hejda" is the most satisfying of the group of character sketches included in this collection. There is a range and perspective to the piece unusual in Nin's writing, and closely akin to Lawrence's methods in his short stories and novels. Based on the pseudonymous "Moira" of Diaries III and IV, "Hejda" is a parable about the difficulties of growth for the modern woman. The opening lines of the story summarize the theme: "The unveiling of women is a delicate matter. It will not happen overnight. We are all afraid of what we shall find" (86). Although Nin explains Hejda's situation rather than dramatically demonstrating it—a defect common to her writing—there is a detached irony to this story unusual in the collection.

Hejda begins as a child of the Orient reared on veils and innuendoes, with a streak of cruelty thrown in besides. Beneath her veils, she was a "little primitive" as a child, walking about without underclothes, torturing frogs and classmates. When she leaves the Orient at seventeen, she "retained an air of being veiled." Like June of the Diary, and Sabina of the fiction, she is mysterious, seductive, sending out erotic signals from her elegantly disguised eyes. She wishes to be noticed as well as to become an artist, and toward those ends she attends art school, decorated with her "aesthetic plumage." Her fellow art student Molnar is captivated by her air of mystery and her plumage. The two of them marry and hide together from the world in their small apartment with one window looking out on a garden. Molnar does not approve of Hejda's voluptuous breasts, and so begins the man's refashioning of the woman in his image. "The drama of woman's development is very painful," Nin comments in relation to Moira in Diary III, "for in each case the man seems to punish all growth. So the woman intent on growth chooses a yielding, passive man who will not interfere with this growth, with her evolution. But in the end, his weakness destroys her" (234).

Eventually, Hejda breaks out of the "stilted, windowless" life she has shared with Molnar. She begins to expand outwardly, to compensate for the compression of her personality experienced in this relationship. Several friends help her "unwind the binding wrapped around her personality first by the family life, then by the husband" (94). Her repressed sexuality comes to the surface. She starts to dress and speak like the "stripteaser, with a slight arrogance, the *agent provocateur*." Her canvases grow larger, as does her personality, but she is "swelling without growing." Hejda is "inflated physically and spiritually," inflated with an unnatural sense of her own importance, with a need to prove her superiority to others, especially women. "Her friendships with women are simply one long underground rivalry" (95), but the underlying cause of this is not explored.

Ironically, this story which began with a promise of growth and change ends with a regression to Hejda's childhood, much as "The Labyrinth" does. "She is back in the garden of her childhood," cruel beneath her veils, confined despite her apparent liberation. Unveiling is a dangerous activity, according to this tale, as growth has destructive potentialities for the modern woman.

"Under a Glass Bell"

Ultimately, all of the characters in *Bell* fail, like Hejda, to break out of the confinements of the self. They may appear to move, as does the narrator on the houseboat, but progress is illusory. The veils remain intact, the labyrinth the preferential form. Vision eludes them, despite promising images such as "The All-Seeing" and "The Eye's Journey." The characters in both these tales see nothing beyond themselves, and that only dimly; they are trapped in their obsessions and illusions. Madness is not far off for "The All-Seeing," it strikes the artist in "The Eye's Journey," and most severely the surrealist artist based on Artraud in "Je Suis Le Plus Malades Des Surrealistes," who is incarcerated in an asylum at the end, babbling with bound feet about the white phoenix and the black eagle.

They are all "Under a Glass Bell," as is Jeanne in the title piece.[7] Isolated, feeding off dreams and the past, Jeanne, like the rest of the characters, remains to the end incapable of removing the transparent container which keeps her confined. This is a continuation of the situation in *House,* as Jeanne is a carry-over from that volume. As before, Jeanne remains hypnotized by her incestuous longings, only in this case she has two brothers rather than one, but no interest in earthly contact with either. She feels she has no body, but an "external envelope" which deludes others into thinking she is still alive. Like Nin of the childhood Diary, she associates herself with Joan of Arc but complains she has "no role to play . . . nothing to save." In the mirror she sees only the "face of the actress," a persistent problem in Nin's writing. The fantasy of being able to "smash the mirror and be one" is as futile as ever.

Nin and some of her critics believe the glass bell is removed in the more realistic pieces, such as "The Mouse" and "Ragtime," but this is not truly the case. "Ragtime" is a charming little piece about the ragpicker's colony the narrator visits one day (as Nin records doing in the Diary). The ragpicker who is the purported subject of this story is actually the mere backdrop for Nin's development of her autobiographical theme. The ragpicker who seeks the "broken, the worn, the faded, the fragmented" is analogous, of course, to the diarist who utilizes the fragments of her life to weave the tapestry of her work, ever incomplete. "What could one do with a complete object," (or a complete art work) the author asks rhetorically. "Put it in a museum," she answers derisively. The narrator wanders through the ragpicker's colony, wondering

if she is in fragments also. "Am I complete? Arms? Legs? Hair? Eyes?
Where is the sole of my foot? . . . Glued to my sole is a blue rag" (60).
The blue rag turns out to be a remnant of her past, the blue dress she wore
to a dance at seventeen. She tries to put it on, but it no longer fits. She is
"forever out of the blue dress," out of her past, but this "blue rag" is
glued to her "sole."

"Can't throw anything away forever," she laments, as she does in her
role as autobiographer. "Nothing is lost but it changes," is the response,
"the new not new / the new not new" (61–62). Despite this theme of
transformation, nothing changes in this story or the pieces in *Bell* as a
whole. The writer finds fragments of herself in the most unlikely
locations. "Ragtime" works as a brief meditation on the author's
methods of composition, of piecing together fragments of her life, but as
a social portrait of the ragpicker's colony it is not particularly persuasive.

"The Mouse" is a sketch of Nin's houseboat maid as well as testimony
to the writer's social consciousness, according to Nin's views, but the
woman under study is treated with a patronizing tone, a gentle ridicule
which hardly yields a sympathetic portrait of an ordinary woman. Nin
refers to the woman throughout the story as "the Mouse," seemingly
unaware of the dehumanization which results from her continual use of
this demeaning epithet. She depicts "the Mouse" as scurrying around the
houseboat, burying away little stolen treasures, getting herself pregnant,
involving her mistress in a sordid abortion. The narrator's role is, of
course, above reproach, generous to a fault, but the epithet "the Mouse"
says it all. The glass bell still presides here.

Chapter Seven
Cities of the Interior:
Voyage toward Daylight

Critical Differences

Cities of the Interior, Nin's five-volume novel series published over a fifteen-year period between 1946 and 1961,[1] is her most ambitious literary project outside the Diary. Conceived as a lengthy experimental novel on the order of Proust's *Remembrance of Things Past,* this series of novellas includes, in final form, *Ladders to Fire, Children of the Albatross, The Four-Chambered Heart, A Spy in the House of Love,* and *Seduction of the Minotaur.*[2] Nin wanted to create a modernist work in *Cities* that would be the verbal equivalent of Duchamp's *Nude Descending a Staircase,* a multiple portrait of modern woman—fragmented, unsure, in the process of self-discovery. Her intention is clearer than her achievement.

Critical reaction to the "continuous novel," as Nin calls it, ranges from Sharon Spencer's declaration that it is a "masterpiece," an "arresting and original synthesis of life in art,"[3] to the more frequent claim that the novels are formless, the characters and plot, beneath the abstract verbiage, reminiscent of soap opera. While Bettina Knapp declares Nin a "Renaissance artist" in *Cities,* working at the height of her artistic powers to create a "veritable orchestration of the senses that imposes a vast new world upon the reader,"[4] Frank Baldanza criticizes the "erratic and baffling" handling of characters and incidents, the "insensitivity to syntax and to canons of usage," as well as the "pointless, rambling" form of the novels.[5] Although *Cities* is a fascinating work from the standpoint of Nin's cumulative self-portrait, from an aesthetic viewpoint it is problematic.

The Diary Connection

The connection between Nin's continuous novel and her Diary is an apparent one. Passages from the published journal appear in the fiction with little or no alteration. Recognizable Diary characters present themselves in *Cities,* but in this interior city they have the poetic license to

make love, albeit in an abstract fashion, whereas in the exposed milieu of
the Diary there are only hints and guesses. "Here one is clothed in the
symbols, protected by the mystery from being completely exposed to the
world" (IV, 73), Nin explains in the context of accounting for her
enigmatic writing.

Not content with her hiding place, Nin must "lift a corner of the veil"
and motion us in, as she does in the Diary. "I am all the women in the
novels, yet still another *not* in the novels" (176), she tosses out in a letter
in Diary IV. "The necessity for fiction was probably born of the problem
of taboo on certain revelations," she explains in *Novel of the Future* (155),
encouraging the reader to turn to the fiction for the "hidden" story of her
life omitted from the Diary. The fiction is, then, a retreat from the
transparently autobiographical nature of the journal to a literary shelter,
a "mantle of protection," and at the same time, a form of disclosure.

Nin had grown accustomed to speaking in the dark through the voice
of her Diary persona, filtering impressions through the sieve of her
journal. The diary-writing habit did not necessitate communication
with the world, any more than it forced self-confrontation. The tendencies toward self-absorption and self-idealization fostered over a lifetime
of journal-keeping manifest themselves in the fictional offspring Nin
produced. Ordinary reality is almost entirely missing from this interior
city, as are the usual trappings of fictional form. Plot and characterization are both treated as variable matters, subject to change without
notice. Structure always was a problem for Nin, but in the Diary it was not
necessary that she overcome it, whereas in the novel series it is a far more
troublesome matter. The novels are formless, held together, like the
Diary, only by the tenuous thread of the writer's projected personality.

Woman's Struggle to Understand Her Own Nature

In the prologue to the first volume, *Ladders to Fire,* published in the
original 1946 edition but not subsequently reprinted, Nin sheds light
on her original intentions in composing her continuous novel. "It is
necessary to return to the origin of confusion," she explains, "which is
woman's struggle to understand her own nature."[6] *Cities of the Interior* is
Nin's attempt to comprehend her own nature which generalizes, to some
extent, to the rest of her sex. According to the writer, the reason woman
has "not been able to organize her own nature" is because "she lacked the
eye of consciousness. She was nature. Man did not help her in this
because his interpretations, whether psychological, or intellectual, or

artistic, did not seize her. And she could not speak for herself." Although Nin appears to accept stereotypic notions of the feminine here, as in the Diary, her goal in *Cities* is to overcome the constraints which prevent her from speaking "for herself," to transcend the nightmare which appears in the first volume: "Anguish was a voiceless woman screaming in a nightmare" (*LF,* 17). Nin searches for her own voice in *Cities* through "multiple exposures of woman's personality." She compartmentalizes herself into three major characters—Lillian, Sabina, and Djuna—and attempts through this three-dimensional character study to piece together a composite identity.

Despite Nin's assertion that woman is "nature," unconscious and unable to speak for herself, her character Djuna embodies the exact opposite of this description. She is the "eye of awareness," yet feminine and highly stylized. Djuna is an ideal conceived by a writer who believes determinedly in wo/man's "infinite possibilities" for growth. Lillian, on the other hand, is the personification of the more limited human reality—"woman as nature"—unconscious, blind to her own nature.

In Lawrentian fashion, Nin mourns woman's loss of "contact with her nature and her relation to man" in the process of entering the spheres of "action and creation." Lillian is presented in *Ladders* as a dramatization of this loss of contact with woman's femininity, since she is introduced as masculine and aggressive, suffering for her active role in love, unable to articulate her grievances. Although Nin does not show us Lillian entering the world of "action and creation," we discover rather belatedly that she is a pianist. But it is her active role in love rather than creation that is concentrated upon as the source of her difficulties.

After an initial involvement with a ghostly lover which quickly ends in frustration, Lillian is smitten by Djuna, the feminine ideal, who offers her a means of self-definition. The homoerotic component in this relationship, as in the one between Lillian and Sabina later in this volume, may be the chief source of the inner battle to which Nin refers in the prologue: "Man appears only partially in this volume, because for the woman at war with herself, he can only appear thus, not as an entity. Woman at war with herself, has not yet been related to man, only to the child in man, being capable only of maternity." In various ways, each of the three central characters is at war with herself, and none of them relate to other than the "child in man" for the duration of the continuous novel.

A full-bodied portrait of an adult man never does materialize, although partially drawn figures of varying degrees of three-dimensionality do appear. The same is true for the women: they are all

half-drawn characters, ever in the process of completion, as Nin suggests
at the end of the prologue: "The mirrors in the garden are the mirrors
women must look into before they can go further. This is only the story
of the mirrors and nature in opposition, and in the mirrors is only what
woman dares to see . . . so far an incomplete woman." It is only at the
conclusion of the last volume that Lillian finally dares to look into the
mirror, and what she sees is a "masked woman, Lillian herself, the
hidden masked part of herself unknown to her, who had ruled her acts"
(*SM*, 111). At the end of *Cities,* as at the beginning, the closest Nin
comes to capturing woman's nature is through her exploration of this
"masked woman" whose reflection can be glimpsed periodically in these
pages.

Voyage without Compass

In the midst of a series of sentence fragments with which *Children of the
Albatross* concludes, Nin declares, "there are those who feared to be lost
in this voyage without compass, barometers, steering wheel or encyclo-
pedias. . ." (173). This phrase serves both as a challenge to the reader
fearful or tired of this "voyage without compass," and an apt description
of the form of the continuous novel. *Cities* takes us on a vast circular
voyage, as in the Diary—without compass or steering wheel. "The cities
of the interior were like the city of Fez," Nin tells us in *Children,*
"intricate, endless, secret and unchartable" (147). Although Nin's novel
series is "unchartable" in terms of traditional plot structure, certain
themes and voices recur, providing continuity in this seemingly plotless
expedition.

The word "compass" is one of the recurrent leitmotivs in the series.
Not only is this a "voyage without compass," but it is a "compass
pointing to mirages." Nin utilizes this phrase in reference to Sabina's
tendency to "murder the present by the dream." The same difficulty
afflicts Djuna who is disconnected from the actual by her propensity to
dream, to barricade herself within a fantasy world. All three women
characters share a tendency to shield themselves from reality with
"mirages," to welcome the "mantle of protection" offered by disguises,
in Sabina's case, by relationships, in Lillian's case, or by a magical inner
world, in Djuna's case. While they all cocoon themselves in a variety of
ways from "naked unbearable truths," they are also terrified of stagnation or stasis. The tension between these two impulses is one of the forces
which propels this voyage along.

Sabina, for example, suffers from a secret sickness, "this fear of stasis," but at the same time, she requires the haven offered her by her husband, her "guardian angel." She is restless and dispersed, playing endless roles, donning a multitude of disguises for her various lovers, but always she returns to her compass, her husband, who offers her solace and comfort after her amorous expeditions (unbeknownst to him). Nin does not explore the contradiction in Sabina's behavior, although she does criticize Jay—personification of Henry Miller in the fiction—for requiring Lillian's love as his "compass" in order to make his freedom possible.

Lillian and Sabina both yearn for this "fixed point in space" which is their steady man, but both become afflicted with restlessness when fixed turn to static dimensions. For Sabina, her husband was a "photograph in her mind, with the static pose which categorized him" (*SHL,* 15), and for Lillian her son did not seem real, any more than her husband, but a "snapshot of Paul taking off his boots . . . her husband's face . . . a photograph too" (*LF,* 25). While in *Ladders* and *Seduction,* Lillian seeks escape from this husband and house which frame and stifle her in a past no longer congruent with who she is, in *Spy* Sabina never does relinquish the shelter of her protective sanctuary. Her need is no doubt greater, since she is the most dispersed of the characters, the most in need of a compass.

Toward the end of *Spy,* Nin comments about Sabina, "The wild compass whose fluctuations she had always obeyed, making for tumult and motion in place of direction, was suddenly fractured so that she no longer knew even the relief of ebbs and flows and dispersions. She felt lost. The dispersion had become too vast, too extended. A shaft of pain cut through the nebulous pattern" (111). The reader might share Sabina's confusion at this point in the novel series, since the "nebulous pattern" of the work leads to this same sensation of a "dispersion . . . too vast, too extended." Perhaps for this reason Nin attempts to tie the disparate threads of *Cities* together in the final volume *Seduction,* but inevitably the last novella returns in a circular direction to certain obsessive themes and concerns evident from the start.

Woman as Artist

All three women characters are artists—Lillian a pianist, Sabina an actress, and Djuna a dancer and presumably a writer. Despite this fact, there is almost no attention given in *Cities* to the demands of their art or the conflicts of being a woman artist. This is somewhat surprising considering the importance of this theme in the Diary, but comprehensible given the fragmentary, abstract treatment of the characters. In the case of Lillian, we learn only belatedly and through the male artist, Jay, that she is a pianist, as if in confirmation of the woman's secondary status vis à vis the male artist in Nin's view at this time. We are told that she had "given up playing in order to work for Jay's support. She had surrendered any hope of becoming a concert pianist to attend better to their immediate needs" (*LF*, 63–64). She is the stereotypic woman once again, sacrificing her own work as an artist to attend to their "immediate needs," and to worship at the shrine of male genius.

In one other scene in *Ladders*, Lillian's role as an artist comes into play. At the conclusion of "This Hunger," the first section of the novella, Lillian is giving a concert in a golden salon, but her playing is of secondary importance in a scene with grander ambitions, as we shall see. Nin does refer to Lillian's frustration with her art, her desperate attempt to attain some form of release through her playing not achievable in her intimate life. Aesthetics are not the issue for Lillian: "She was not playing to throw music into the blue space, but to reach some climax, some impossible union with the piano. . . . She pounded the coffer of the piano as she wanted her own body pounded and shattered. And the pain on her face was that of one who reached neither sainthood nor pleasure. No music rose and passed out of the window, but a sensual cry, heavy with unspent forces" (79). Lillian is blocked artistically and sexually, unable to reach a state of self-forgetfulness, an "impossible union" in either sphere. But there is no further development of this theme. Lillian is no longer depicted as sexually blocked in *Seduction*, the last volume, which focuses on her once again.

In *Seduction*, Lillian travels to Golcando to play piano in a nightclub, but her role as pianist is immaterial in this volume, aside from Nin's comment that her lack of discipline had hampered her achievement. This same lack of discipline is mentioned in reference to Rango, the guitarist, in *Heart*, Jay the painter in *Ladders*, and Sabina the amateur actress in *Spy*. Jay suggests this about Sabina: "But when he pressed her he could not find in what play she had acted, whether she had been a success or a failure, whether, perhaps, (as he decided later) she had merely *wished* to be an actress but had never worked persistently enough, seriously enough except in the way she was working now, changing personalities with such rapidity that Jay was reminded of a kaleidoscope" (122). Sabina lacks discipline as an artist because the craft involved in being an actress is not her concern: it is the role alone which preoccupies her.

Her part as an actress is more vital to her characterization than are the artistic roles of Lillian or Djuna because she never ceases to be an actress—in life, not on stage. She pretends to be an actress in order to escape from her husband and to have liaisons with a series of casual strangers. She is also addicted to her continually changing disguises and knows no other existence. As a result, she has become "lost . . . somewhere along the frontier between her inventions, her stories, her fantasies and her true self.

The boundaries had become effaced, the tracks lost; she had walked into pure chaos, and not a chaos which carried her like the galloping of romantic riders in operas and legends, but which suddenly revealed the stage props: A papiêr-maché horse" (111). Behind her actor's mask—a papiêr-maché prop—she has ceased to exist, as was the case with Stella.

Nin is noticeably more convincing in her characterization of Sabina as actress and personality than she is with Lillian or Djuna. She is, in a sense, the key to Nin's style, as well as to the mysteries of the "hidden self" in Nin's writing. Some of the most effective passages which summarize Sabina's traits are repeated in both *Ladders* and *Spy*, confirming their importance to the work as a whole. "The faces and the figures of her personages appeared only half drawn," we are told, "and when one just began to perceive them another face and figure were interposed, as in a dream. . ." (*LF*, 110). This is exactly what happens in *Ladders:* just as we begin to form a picture of Lillian and Jay—despite the sketchiness of their portraits—the scene changes and the names Djuna and Jay appear. Similarly, "She was impelled by a great confessional fever which forced her to lift a corner of the veil, but became frightened if anyone listened or peered at the exposed scene, and then she took a giant sponge and rubbed it all out, to begin somewhere else, thinking that in confusion there was protection. So Sabina beckoned and lured one into her world, and then blurred the passageways, confused the images and ran away in fear of detection" (*LF*, 110). Just so Nin utilizes an obfuscatory style as a means of protection, yet she lures one into her world with her "confessional fever." The dual impulses of concealment and exposure characterize Nin's style as well as Sabina.

Djuna is a far more abstract character than Sabina; she is the most remote and idealized of the three, and hence the closest to Nin's ideal Diary persona. If Sabina is the notorious id, anarchic, impulsive, and perverse, and Lillian the ego, the flawed human being, Djuna is certainly the ego ideal or superego.[7] But these categories are no more fixed in this novel series than they are in life. Djuna's idealized status dissolves as the continuous novel progresses. What sets Djuna apart is her magical inner chamber—fictional equivalent of the Diary—in which she transforms "naked unbearable truths" to a form no longer lethal. She is immune from the human frailties exhibited by the other characters, to a large extent, because of her powerful weapon against despair.

By the conclusion of *Ladders*, however, her ideal position has been eroded since her remote and idealized status separates her from human life. Her inner chamber is now described as the "glass bastions of her city of the interior," making clear both her confinement from real life, and the centrality of her position in this interior city, since her inner chamber and the "city of the interior" are now synonymous. She is the creator of this novel series symbolically, the writer's eye of perception, at the same time as she is a participant in the drama, struggling with the same human limitations as the others. In the final party sequence in *Ladders*, this becomes apparent when she begs for someone to release her from her "glass bastions." "Bring me one who knows that the dream without exit, without explosion, without awakening, is the passageway to the world of the dead! I want my dress torn and stained!" (151). But her plea is not answered; instead, someone brings her a gold chair, a "hierarchic offering" which condemns her to her idealized status.

Fragmentation and Multiplicity

"There is something broken inside of me," cries Djuna in *Children*. Sabina and Lillian also suffer from sensations of fragmentation and self-division. The problem is accentuated when one of the characters is made aware of the disparity between the masked facade, designed to please the world, and the interior self, invariably less noble and more chaotic than the exterior might indicate. In *Heart* Nin tells us that Djuna "felt much less good than she was expected to be. It gave her a feeling of treachery, of deception" (82). This good self is described as an "artificial bloom" which now had its "devotees" and "compulsive life," making abandonment of the role difficult if not impossible. "This goodness is a role, too tight around me," Djuna complains, "it is a costume I can no longer wear" (85).

Djuna also has the tendency to compartmentalize her personality in order to avoid the painful side of life. "Partitioning," Nin tells us, is "one of the great secrets against shattering sorrows" (*CA*, 28). But this propensity can also lead to inner fragmentation, dispersion of the self into a myriad pieces. Sabina is the character most in danger of disintegration into a thousand fragments, as Nin observes in *Spy:* "there was no Sabina, not ONE, but a multitude of Sabinas lying down yielding and being dismembered, constellating in all directions and breaking. A small Sabina who felt weak at the center carried on a giant wave of dispersion." (109).

At times Nin bemoans this sense of fragmentation and weakness "at the center," but other times she accepts it as part of the modern notion of personality. In *Heart* Djuna comments upon the many roles which compose the self called "Djuna," including the roles she plays in her dreams—which Sabina embodies in her waking life. Djuna acknowledges her identification with Sabina's dream sequences, thereby challenging the notion of her personality originally presented (a sign of the author's flexibility or inconsistency, depending upon your viewpoint). "Beneath the cities of the interior," Nin remarks a bit later, "flowed many rivers carrying a multitude of images. . . . All the women she had been spread their hair in a halo on the surface of the river, extended multiple arms like the idols of India. . ." (178). Nin seems to find in this notion of multiplicity a solution for the dispersion and fragmentation evident in her characters.

She utilizes Duchamp's famous painting, *Nude Descending a Staircase,* as a keynote of this theme of multiplicity as a fact of modern life. Djuna comments on the "movement of the many layers of the self" in the painting which do not flow "in one direction" any more than do the aspects of a given personality. In *Spy* it is Sabina who recognizes herself in the painting: "Eight or ten outlines of the same woman, like many multiple exposures of a woman's personality, neatly divided into many layers, walking down the stairs in unison" (127). In Sabina's case, each outline of a woman plays a role in relation to a given lover. "If she went to Alan now," Nin elaborates, "it would be like detaching one of these cutouts of a woman, and forcing it to walk separately from the rest, but once detached from the unison, it would reveal that it was a mere outline of a woman, the figure design as the eye could see it, but empty of substance, this substance having evaporated through the spaces between each layer of the personality. A divided woman indeed, a woman divided into numberless silhouettes. . ." (127–28). Through her development of this motif, Nin both provides a rationale for her contradictory and role-playing characters and a warning of the dangers of excessive role diffusion—namely, the possibility that the woman who plays too many roles may become "empty of substance" beneath her facade.

Mirrors and the Garden

Ladders to Fire, despite the fragmentation and confusion of plot and characterization, contains two of the most intriguing, enigmatic scenes in the continuous novel. They are both set pieces, cardboard "cut-outs" which protrude from the text, as the characters are the same. Their appeal may derive in part from their incompletion; they are not fully prepared for or sustained, nor can we be certain of their meaning, since they are highly condensed and abstracted.

The first scene involves Djuna and Jay who are linked in an intimate setting without explanation. Previously, we had been acquainted with Lillian and Jay and now, with no forewarning, these two are placed in conjunction, as if to throw us off the track. Djuna is at the center of this scene. She stands before her mirror perfuming herself while Jay admires her from the couch, assuring her of her significance in his self-conception. "I have grown used to considering your image of me as the correct one," he tells her. "I was like a wheel without a hub" (68). Much as Lillian looked to Jay for her self-conception, so Jay turns to Djuna for his "correct" image; only Djuna seems immune to such dependency. She is the hub of Jay's life, we are told without demonstration, as she is the hub of the novel series, but she is also fixed in her position at the center of the wheel. "I could swear the garden is made of cardboard," Jay comments. "You are almost transparent there, like the mist of perfume you are throwing on yourself. Throw more perfume on yourself, like a fixative on a water color" (68). Djuna responds with what Nin calls an "immense distress quite out of proportion to his fancy." "You don't quite believe in me as a woman," she complains, apparently disturbed at the implication of her artificiality.

Immediately afterward, the scene shifts to a series of abstractions—extremely condensed, almost willfully obfuscatory. Nin likens the color of the day to the "color of Byzantine paintings," a "soft powdery gold which seemed on the verge of decomposing," as Djuna's personality is perhaps on the verge of disintegrating in response to Jay's observations. What Nin focuses upon is the "fibrous space lying behind the illusion, the absence of color and depth, the condition of emptiness and blackness underneath the gold powder. This gold powder which had fallen now on the garden" (69). The implication is that Djuna, like Sabina and Stella, is in danger of evaporating beneath her illusory appearance, since it is only her gold facade which is recognized by others, such as Jay. The human and natural have been lost; even the garden is now coated with gold powder.

"The essence, the human essence always evaporating where the dream installed itself and presided" (69). The present, the "human essence" has been destroyed by her penchant for dreams and idealization. Immediately after this sentence, Nin switches again without warning to Lillian, producing confusion in the reader, questions about the extent of Nin's artistic control over her text, and the distinct impression that unpleasant revelations lead to a sudden change in direction in the plot.

The final scene in "This Hunger" opens with Lillian giving a concert in a golden salon (continuing the gold motif), with floors so highly polished there are "two Lillians, two pianos, two audiences." One Lillian is the human being with her pent-up sexual frustrations, already described, while the other is no doubt her idealized counterpart, Djuna, who sits in her customary pose of detachment on the "borderline between the perfumed crowd and the silent, static garden" (80). Djuna's eyes catch the garden "as if in a secret exposure," and what is exposed is an "air of nudity,"

a sensual humidity as if leaves, trees, grass and wind were all in a state of caress. . . . The eyes of the people inside could not bear the nudity of the garden, its exposure. The eyes of the people had needed the mirrors, delighted in the fragility of reflections. All the truth of the garden, the moisture, and the worms, the insects and the roots, the running sap and the rotting bark, had all to be reflected in the mirrors. . . . Art and artifice had breathed upon the garden and the garden had breathed upon the mirror, and all the danger of truth and revelation had been exorcised. (80–81)

What Djuna's eyes catch in a "secret exposure" is the hidden text of Nin's writing which has a similar "air of nudity," both in its revelatory and seductive aspects. The sensual climate which surrounds "This Hunger" and all the novellas is the same climate which surrounds the Diary, but Djuna, the transformer of "unbearable truths" in her inner chamber, realizes the need for mirrors, for art and artifice in the telling: "The eyes of the people inside could not bear the nudity of the garden, its exposure" (81). No longer concerned about the "condition of emptiness and blackness beneath the gold powder," Nin through Djuna, appears reconciled in this concluding piece to the necessity for artifice in the writing. The dangers of truth and revelation in this autobiographical writing are "exorcised" by a mystifying prose style which is here rationalized as a necessary protection both for the audience and the artist. The writer needs it for protection from judgment, and the readers because they could not handle more transparent revelations.

But, in fact, the dangers are not all "exorcised," as Nin points out in the conclusion: "Under the house and under the garden there were subterranean passages and if no one heard the premonitory rumblings before the explosion, it would all erupt in the form of war and revolution. The humiliated, the defeated, the oppressed, the enslaved. Woman's misused and twisted strength" (81). Nin warns of the revolutionary potential of women in particular, with their "misused and twisted strength," at the same time as she implies the disruptive potential of the "subterranean passages" in her text which are also kept from view. In the remainder of *Cities,* however, the "subterranean passages" which do surface are hiding places more than revolutionary rumblings. Djuna and Lillian both turn to their underground tunnels for protection. They enact their rebellions through others, such as Jay and Rango. The tendency toward retreat and evasion is far more distinct in *Cities* after the first volume than the possibility of explosive upheaval of any sort.

Ladders to Fire

Lillian and Sabina are the characters with the most disruptive potential in *Cities,* with Sabina, the incendiary influence above all. From her first introduction in *Ladders* to her novel, *Spy,* she is associated with the "sound and imagery of fire engines." She is a warning signal, a destructive force, and a creature of passionate intensity—"The first time one looked at Sabina one felt: everything will burn!" (*LF,* 108). Sabina is the secret self beneath the mask of the perfect woman artist, represented by Djuna. She enacts in daytime, as Djuna declares in *Heart,* what other women dare only in their dreams. She is a step further than Lillian, leading her on to more conspicuous acts of rebellion against society's established patterns. Both Lillian and Sabina are rebels of sorts; they defy traditional notions of how women should act. Sabina plays Don Juana in *Spy,* even if not entirely successfully, and Lillian acts the aggressor in love when she is first introduced in *Ladders.* They have an element of perversity in their personalities which Nin elaborates upon in *Ladders,* although not thereafter.

After Lillian has a brief courtship with a ghostly male lover named Gerard whom she appears to have dreamt more than met, she retreats in injury from this shadow play declaring, "If woman plays the Don Juan and does the courting and the man retreats she is mutilated in some way" (21). Lillian turns away from men temporarily after this experience, becomes a "warrior," and focuses her romantic impulses on a female phantom instead, Djuna, who answers her dream of what she herself would like to be. Djuna is no more tangible as a character than Gerard, but the intimacy between them is more convincingly portrayed. They both express the fervent wish that the other were a man.

Djuna acts as guide and guardian to Lillian, much as the writer does to Sabina in *House* and Nin to June Miller in Diary I. Instead of retracting at Lillian's advances, Djuna plays a responsive and supportive role, clarifying Lillian's half-understood impressions. "How long will woman be ashamed of her strength?" (21) she asks rhetorically; the novella suggests it will be a long while. Lillian ceases to be "ashamed of her strength" with Djuna, but other difficulties intervene in this intimacy. Lillian becomes possessive and clinging, all human but uncommendable attributes, whereas Djuna's behavior is above reproach, indicating her idealized status. She wishes only to illuminate and support Lillian, and perhaps to enjoy her rebelliousness vicariously. The disintegration of this relationship is not fully explained, any more than the sudden abandonment of Lillian's home and family.

Lillian continues to become infatuated with other women in *Ladders*, a bit later with Helen, again with Sabina in "Bread and the Wafer," the second part of *Ladders*. The description of these involvements is quite similar, although the one between Lillian and Sabina is closest to Nin and June Miller in Diary I. There is a vivid description of the two women dancing in a nightclub and being jeered at by the men. "They wanted to break the walls confining them, suffocating them. They wanted to break out from the prison of their own fears, break every obstacle. But all they found to break were glasses" (121). They break the glasses over their shoulders and are thrown out of the club, but this defiant act does not help them break out of the guilt and fear confining them. Shortly thereafter, the two of them finally manage to touch, but almost immediately pull away: "They separated and saw it was not this they wanted, sought, dreamed. Not this the possession they imagined. No bodies touching would answer this mysterious craving in them to become each other" (125).

Nin returns to this same interpretation of the intimacy between Lillian and Sabina at the end of *Cities*, apparently bothered by the homoerotic implications of her tale, as she seems to be in Diary I. The conclusion she reaches—that this homoerotic infatuation was not lesbianism but a form of narcissism, a desire to make the self more complete—may well be correct, but it does not fully account for the intensity of emotion apparent in the passages involving two women.

Homoeroticism is one of the "subterranean" themes beneath the mystifying and fragmented surface of this novel. It is one of the ladders which leads to fire.

Heterosexual love is, however, equally problematic, as was indicated in the abortive romance between Lillian and Gerard, and is further demonstrated in the difficult love between Lillian and Jay. Just as Miller is the most complete male character in the Diary, so Jay is the most three-dimensional male character in *Cities,* even if he, too, remains incomplete. As in the Diary, what is emphasized here about this "gnome and sprite and faun" is his ability, enviable to Lillian, to enter life fully and enjoy it with ease and intense pleasure. Lillian is transformed by this relationship, to such an extent that it is almost impossible to recognize in this new Lillian the character from the first part of the novel. The rebellious woman who had given up husband and children seemingly without a second thought now becomes domestic and protective, "sewing their days together," offering him "shelter and refuge." The assertiveness which had been a problem with men formerly ceases to be an issue; instead, Lillian suffers because of her overdependence on Jay. She looks to him to define and create her, builds her days around his departures and returns to their love nest.

As "Bread and the Wafer" progresses, however, it becomes clear that Lillian cannot thrive in the shadow of Jay's personality or art. Her own identity, as is often the case for women, "dissolves" in his presence. She had imagined that he—the male artist genius—"would set her free," as she had dreamt that Djuna would save her. The extent of his productivity and desires, his craving for new experiences, and unwillingness to protect her from his sordid escapades all break down her sacrificial love. Finally she concludes that he is incapable of turning inward or of comprehending the subtleties of her personality. In her distress at these realizations, she turns to Djuna who summarizes in a detached fashion the fallacy of Lillian's yearnings: "Lillian, no one should be entrusted with one's image to fashion, with one's self-creation. Women are moving from one circle to another, rising towards independence and self-creation. . . . You know you cannot lean on Jay, but you don't know what awaits you, and you don't trust your own awareness" (133). Love, for Lillian, may be a form of transcendence, but it also means a crippling dependency which destroys her chances for self-creation. Guilt and fear are the destructive fires through which she must pass if self-renewal is to come about, but there is no clear resolution of the matter.

How Can One Liquidate the Past?

"How can one liquidate the past?" This question, raised by one of the characters in *Ladders*, echoes throughout the five novels. Despite the futility of the effort, the three women characters attempt exactly this—through adolescent men in *Children*, through the drug of illusory romantic love in *Heart*, through nymphomania in *Spy*, through the drug of forgetfulness in *Seduction*. Djuna, Sabina, and Lillian are all fugitives from the labyrinth of the past they would prefer to escape but cannot.

Sabina, in *Spy*, is "in flight, from the guilt of love divided, and from the guilt of not loving" (137). She is pursued by her conscience, personified by the Lie Detector, as Lillian is similarly shadowed by Dr. Hernandez in *Seduction*. Both are engaged in the futile effort to escape awareness of the meaning of their actions. Significantly enough, Nin has the proponent of the drug of awareness rather than oblivion, Dr. Hernandez, killed off in *Seduction*. It is the only death in the continuous novel, suggesting the extent of Nin's ambivalence on the virtues of awareness.

Even Djuna who is supposedly the great eye of perception becomes the mistress of oblivion in *Children*, thriving on the "anaesthetic of the dream" which dulls the pain of living. By immersing herself in the relative harmlessness of the "airy young men," she attempts to avoid self-confrontation. She gives up the "insincere pretense of maturity," as Nin calls it, and loses herself in admiration for their "iridescence" and "phosphorescence"—words used repeatedly in this volume. In fact, the word repetitions are so blatant in *Children* it is difficult to imagine how they could have escaped Nin's attention.

Djuna's motivation for regression in *Children* is explained as an instinctive reaction to memories too painful to bear. The "thread of Ariadne," the same thread followed in the Diary, "began to cut her fingers from unwinding so much." The albatross of this novel's title is perhaps the weight of this preoccupation with the past, and the childhood wound which no efforts at oblivion seem able to eradicate from memory. Even though Nin does not describe the "wound," the ramifications are enumerated, the "swift regressions into her adolescent state," the "muffled" heart "closed hermetically into muteness," the construction of a "veritable fort under this mask of gentle shyness," the same fort constructed by Lillian in *Ladders*.

Nin continues the theme of regression in *Heart*, only in this instance the tactic is withdrawal into the cocoon of romantic love. From the start,

Nin describes the love between Djuna and Rango, a fictional version of
Gonzalo, as a "mirage," but the need for the "great narcotic" of love is
greater than the awareness of its illusory aspects. We are expected to
appreciate Nin's image of Rango "on the open road," symbol of freedom
and desire, even while it is clearly demonstrated that he is a man
hopelessly entangled in defeatism and self-delusion. To make matters
worse, overwriting becomes rampant in this volume, as the first few
paragraphs of the novel suggest:

The guitar distilled its music.
Rango played it with the warm copper color of his skin, with the charcoal pupil
of his eyes, with the underbrush thickness of his eyebrows, pouring into the
honey-colored box the flavors of the open road on which he lived his gypsy life:
thyme, rosemary, oregano, marjoram, and sage. Pouring into the resonant box
the sensual swing of his hammock hung across the gypsy cart and the dreams
born on his mattress of black horsehair. (5–6)

The "great narcotic" of love which Nin attempts to describe in this novel
simply does not work its spell due largely to writing such as this which
surely puts off more readers than it captivates. Unfortunately, the
syntactical awkwardness of the above passage is a regular feature of the
continuous novel, particularly in the middle three volumes. Nin's
oblivousness to style is mirrored in an apparent retreat from awareness in
this volume, as in *Children*.

Despite Nin's repeated claims of Djuna's "extraordinary intensity of
vision," she seems remarkably imperceptive in her involvement with
Rango and Zora, his destructively mad wife. Djuna's dream of Rango's
capacity to break out of his self-imposed trap becomes increasingly unlikely as the novel wears on. Rango is determined to subside into fatality,
with the collaboration of his wife, his coconspirator in refusing to grow or
live. Djuna becomes engaged in attempting to retrieve Rango from this
inevitability partly, no doubt, to fight the fatality in herself. Throughout
Cities there is a tug of war between the belief, expressed by Djuna in
Ladders, that "life tended to crystallize into patterns which became traps
and webs" (28), and a struggle against such patterns.

Lillian runs away to Golconda in *Seduction* specifically to escape the
"traps and webs" of the past, epitomized by her recurrent nightmare of a
"ship that could not reach the water, that sailed laboriously, pushed by
her with great effort, through city streets" (5). Her voyage to this
Mexican seaside resort had its inception, Nin tells us, in her "urgent

need to contradict" this dream. She conceives of the image of a solar barque, after the Egyptian myth, as a symbol of Lillian's new-found mobility, her release from this nightmare of stagnation. Throughout *Seduction,* Nin alludes to the solar barque in testimony of Lillian's changed personality. "Tropics," she reminds us, comes from the Greek meaning "change and turning," and Nin is determined to prove that Lillian has changed.

The Doctor does not for a moment believe her assertions. "Chaos is a convenient hiding place for fugitives," he informs her. "You are a fugitive from truth" (29). Lillian does not appreciate his observations and, perhaps unconsciously, wills him to his early demise. Nin does not hint at this in *Seduction,* however; on the contrary, she suggests that the Doctor might have wished to die himself and was thus a suicide of sorts.

Whatever Nin's assertions about change in *Seduction,* the text reveals this to be another mirage. Each attempt Lillian makes to evade her past leads to a new confrontation with her own familiar patterns. She introduces Fred as an original type, but it becomes quickly apparent he is another in the long line of "airy young men." Diane comes along next and takes her place with the other female "provocateurs." Lillian gets duped into paying for the release of a prisoner who is confined by greed not the law, but this incident makes her realize her attraction to the imprisoned is a reflection of her continued self-confinement. She is a "prisoner of anxiety," a "prisoner of timidities," she admits. Despite her conviction that she has left her past behind her, a visit to an ancient town, silent and static, returns her to early memories. She is a victim of the "double exposure created by memory," the same overlap created in the Diary. Lillian presumably has a powerful revelation toward the end of *Seduction,* but immediately afterward, we are taken on a long "detour of the past" that confirms once again the fact that we have been on a circular expedition.

Nin apparently was at a loss as to how to end her continuous novel, as she records in the Diary. Despite her intention to show change and growth in her characters, she is unclear as to how to bring this about. In Lillian's revelation toward the end of *Seduction,* there is a movement toward daylight, but she is not there yet:

Lillian had felt the existence of the labyrinth beneath her feet like the excavated passageways under Mexico City, but she had feared entering it and meeting the Minotaur who would devour her.

Yet now that she had come face to face with it, the Minotaur resembled someone she knew. It was not a monster. It was a reflection upon a mirror, a masked woman, Lillian herself, the hidden masked part of herself unknown to her, who had ruled her acts. She extended her hand toward this tyrant who could no longer harm her. It lay upon the mirror of the plane's round portholes, traveling through the clouds, a fleeting face, her own, clear and definable only when darkness came. (111)

Chapter Eight
Collages:
We Must Always Smile

Like Lillian Gish in Griffith's silent film classic *Broken Blossoms,* Nobuko, one of the characters in *Collages,* produces a smile only by holding up the corners of her mouth with her index fingers. "We must always smile," she declares, and then mimics a flood of tears, "even when we feel like weeping" (79). This could be the motto for *Collages,* a book which Nin intended to be humorous. The main character, Renate, always smiles even when she feels like weeping, but this is hardly sufficient to produce a humorous book. There are several delightful interludes in this work, but as with the rest of Nin's writing, it is not particularly humorous.

Nin says she wanted the book to be more a "collage or mobile than a full solid work" (NF, 92). She took her inspiration from the surrealists who employed the collage method to such striking effect, especially in the work of Max Ernst or Kurt Schwitters. As in a visual collage, Nin constructed her book through the assemblage of a number of unrelated elements—in this case characters and stories from the Diary. The question is, to what extent does a new meaning emerge from this assemblage, and to what extent is there a controlling artist at work? While there are some new elements in this collection of stories, by and large there are no new themes or ideas introduced. Instead, many of the old motifs are replayed in Nin's swan song to her fiction. There is also no controlling design apparent, no structural organization at work. The book appears, at first, to be about Renate, but she is suddenly dropped approximately one third of the way through the book, only to be picked up thereafter as a name rather than a vital character, as if to create a semblance of continuity. After this point, *Collages* is basically a collection of character sketches, although some of them are strikingly effective.

The characters are the strength of *Collages.* There are a few dozen of them, mostly culled from the Diary, and many resembling the writer. Her most memorable characters are the painter Renate, the collage artist Varda, the old man who lives by the sea and gradually comes to resemble the seals he admires, and the Consul's wife who writes about adventurous women, has a complicated fantasy life, while playing the perfect wife to her Don Juan husband.

Renate is the character who comes closest to holding the book together, in however tenuous a fashion. She is based upon Renate Druks, first introduced in Diary V. In the fiction, she is the one who "must always smile," whereas in the Diary she has occasion to weep with real despair when her son, who becomes a drug addict, dies of an overdose. This son is not included in Collages, although the fact that Renate has a son is mentioned once with no development. Had he been part of Renate's portrait, Collages would certainly have been a different, and perhaps richer, book. While Sharon Spencer believes Renate is "the most fully developed example of Anaïs Nin's concept of femininity and art,"[1] this hardly seems plausible given the fact that she is not "fully developed" as a character. Neither her life nor her art are explored in a particularly profound fashion. She has her role to play as the joyous woman artist who paints animals and women in strange combinations and who tolerates the ambiguous affection of Bruce, her homosexual, narcissistic male companion. We are offered a brief sketch of her childhood in Vienna with her fixation on statues and her father, but hardly enough to produce a full-scale portrait.

Bruce is another in the long line of homosexual males in Nin's writing, leading Oliver Evans to complain that he is "merely another one of the largely unsympathetic portraits in Miss Nin's gallery of half-men."[2] Here, too, we only get a quick sketch of his personality, especially given the quality of his utterances. When Renate first meets him, we are told that her fantasies about the statues help her to understand him, since his speech consists of, "Man, see, man, see here, man, oh man." Although the origin of this attraction between Renate and Bruce is not clarified, the difficulties in their relationship are spelled out quite graphically when Renate accidentally catches a glimpse of Bruce engaged in an intimate combo with a Mexican adolescent male. Renate runs away from this spectacle, attempting to obliterate her pain in a bright orange dress which fails to convince her, although it fools others, that she is now joyous. However, she readily accepts Bruce when he reappears on the scene in Malibu, offering him a peace dove rather than demanding one of him.

The two of them attempt to mend their relationship by sailing around Europe together, but like the other voyages in Nin's writing, this one too proves abortive. Bruce is not a sailor, and Renate is forced to bail them out. After this debacle, Renate's house is threatened by fire and Bruce thinks only of himself, walking away from near-disaster with Renate's painting of him tucked under his arm, while she is left hosing the roof. She still holds on inexplicably, like Djuna in *Heart,* long after the reader has lost sympathy with her fidelity to this relationship. Bruce consoles her with a Chinese puzzle box which he advises her to open whenever she finds his disappearances intolerable. What the box reveals is not only his homosexual and sadomasochistic tendencies, but also his capacity to lie in a situation of panic and cause a Mexican boy to be put in jail to save his own skin. This finally appears to cure Renate of Bruce.

But there are positive male characters in the book, especially Varda, who is also the object of Nin's admiring attention in the Diary. Through him, Nin confirms once again her faith in the transformative powers of art. "Nothing endures," declares the collage artist, "unless it has been transposed into a myth," and this is of course what Nin hoped to do in the translation of her life into her autobiographical art. "His collages taught how to remain in a state of grace," the writer explains, "extract only elixirs, transmute . . . all women, by a process of cut-outs, to aphrodisiacs" (60). Nin, too, is interested in extracting only "elixirs" through a "process of cut-outs" in her life-work. Nin comments that Varda's women are "interchangeable and mobile," as of course Nin's characters are as well, although their mobility is frequently stymied.

The last episode in the book is the most intriguing in the volume. A Dr. Mann, who makes a passionate hobby out of tracking down women writers, is determined to have an audience with the elusive Judith Sands, presumably based on Djuna Barnes, the artist Nin unsuccessfully attempted to contact herself. When Dr. Mann tries to win her over with a monologue outside her door reminiscent of the doctor's monologues in Barnes's *Nightwood,* he might be speaking for Nin: "I feel that, in a sense, you gave birth to me. I feel you once described a man who was *me* before I knew who I was, and it was because I recognized him that I was able to be myself. . . . When you deny me your presence, you commit spiritual murder" (114–115).

Finally he is able to persuade Judith to accompany him to a cultural spectacle at the Museum of Modern Art. They watch as Tinguely's modernist contraption resembling a Louise Nevelson sculpture—an assemblage of odds and ends from the street all painted chalk white—is set up for explosion. Perhaps this is Nin's symbolic bonfire of her own writing since all the elements in this performance reflect back on her work, beginning with the assemblage painted white. Out of this combustible spectacle a paper unrolls with the names of the immortal artists, but the list is perversely withdrawn, swallowed in a "desperate inversion," similar to the endlessly unrolling but inverted pages of Nin's Diary. A child's carriage careens out of the burning heap, (Nin's childhood or childlessness) like the baby carriage in Eisenstein's *Potemkin,* but is "unable to escape." The notes of a piano can be heard, but they are wistful, out of tune, unreal; the music is "trapped . . . hollow, expiring" (like Nin's writing, now coming to an end, and reminiscent of Lillian's problematic playing in *Ladders*). This infernal activity is described as "inverted" and "introverted," both of which apply to Nin's work, "bending and twisting and tearing at itself, introverted activity ending sometimes in a deadlock" (119). The ladder leading to fire falls, thus heralding the end of Nin's fiction writing which began early on with "ladders to fire." The color orange coded with passion in this volume and *Seduction* (Lillian and Renate both wear orange dresses in the tropics) appears in the form of an orange balloon which bursts (as the characters usually cannot, however pent up with desire). The fire chief tries to interfere with this conflagration, as male authority figures are always trying to interfere, from Dr. Hernandez in *Seduction,* to the doctor in "Birth," to Edmund Wilson in Diary IV. But the artist gives the crumbling structure the kick of death, granting him the final word, according to Nin's creed.

Dr. Mann and Judith leave the spectacle after he rescues the roll of paper containing the names of the immortal artists—with Judith Sands's name among them. They cross paths with Renate and Bruce and the four of them return to Judith's apartment, at which point Judith removes from beneath her couch her precious manuscript which turns out to be the opening words of *Collages,* bringing this book, like its predecessors, full circle. Not only has it been proven that "Nothing is ever finished," one of the key lines of the book, but also the link has been clearly established between the immortal Sands and the author of the book, whose own longings for immortality are indirectly conveyed through her story.

Chapter Nine

Conclusion:
Multi-faceted Self-Portrait

Anaïs Nin's greatest achievement was her multi-faceted self-portrait, contained in both her Diary and her experimental fiction. The Diary is by far her more successful literary accomplishment, especially the first two volumes which are Nin's finest works of art. Throughout the Paris Diaries, there are passages of extraordinary brilliance and perception, descriptions of psychic states of confusion and duality, dramatic scenes which captivate and delight us with their candor and charm. The spectacle of Nin's continually changing masks and roles fascinates us, as does the subtle mating dance between Nin, June, and Henry Miller. In June Miller, Nin discovers her greatest subject, her most compelling alter ego, which she also makes the basis of her most effective work of fiction, *House of Incest*.

As the pages accumulate, however, the narcissism evident in Nin's Diary from the start becomes more problematic as the author grows increasingly preoccupied with convincing herself and her readers that she is worthy of such immense attention. The more she utilizes her Diary as a means of defense and persuasion, the less concerned she appears to be with the aesthetic merits of her text. In volumes V and VI this situation is reversed to some extent; Nin makes a determined effort to observe the surrounding world with a sharper eye, to offer skillful portraits of others. But her intention to make her book a "journal of others" is not altogether convincing when the others she summons into her text all appear to be witnesses for the defense, especially in the last volume where the testimonies to Nin's uniqueness overwhelm her book.

However, the two early Diaries published since Nin's death counterbalance this negative last impression, for they are full of a precocity and charming ingenuousness which engage us as the journals of the older Nin often do not. It remains to be seen how the two intermediate volumes yet to be published will effect the overall design and value of the Diary. Until these Diaries are in print and a few more years have passed, Nin's stature will not be decided. Nevertheless, it is clear that the greatest significance of Nin's Diary is in its universality.

In treading the path of her inner labyrinth, her "Inside World," Nin participated in a quest for identity and meaning which brought her into connection with the "Outside World," as she called it in adolescence. She turned herself into the modern heroine who enters the labyrinth of her life-book, as Theseus entered the Cretan labyrinth of old, prepared to struggle with the minotaur of her neurosis, of her own dark fears and desires. The monster of her own self-doubts—her right to write—was perhaps the most formidable. Nonetheless, she persisted on her circular journey despite the imposing obstacles. Her courage was not of course sustained; at times she utilized her "paper womb" as a "protective cave" in which to hide, rather than a method of self-confrontation. But her need for withdrawal and protection humanized her quest, as her interior cave brought her into relation with others, particularly her gender, so long associated with private spheres.

Many of the themes and images which haunted Nin have resonance for countless others, particularly women. Her search for identity through the looking glass and through her changing masks, her sensations of self-division, fragmentation and multiplicity are all widely shared. Perhaps most important, her conflicts and her effort to define herself as a woman artist are part of a female literary tradition. Nin's "anxiety of authorship" is almost universally shared by women writers past if not present. Her struggle between love and creation, duty and self-fulfillment, her guilt for creating and association of writing with masculinity and aggression have been widely reported. The silences which mar her work—the omission of husband and lovers from her Diary—are comprehensible in light of this tradition. Nin was born at the end of the Victorian era, subject to the same repressive forces which stifled Woolf and many more.

The defects in Nin's work cannot all, however, be eradicated from this viewpoint. Her difficulty in seeing others as well as herself without distortion or a romantic patina is an individual matter. Nin was reluctant to come to grips with the painful side of reality, with unattractive aspects of human nature, especially her own. This human enough deficiency can be fatal to an autobiographer, as can the tendency to self-idealization also apparent in the Diary. Like her father, Nin was too dazzled by her own reflection, and not fascinated enough by the infinite variety of humanity, except in the form of worthy artistic subjects to be won over, captured in her book. She tended to discount the importance of aesthetic matters in part because of her agreement with the surrealist and psychoanalytic emphasis on free association and spontaneity. As a result, her style is noticeably uneven, with passages of precision and beauty, especially in her early writing, but others that are stockpiled with nouns and adjectives which do not yield the results Nin intended. Repetitions abound in the Diary; many of the same incidents and phrases appear in the sixth Diary as in the fifth, and the same is true in *Cities of the Interior*. Nin's carelessness about syntax also undermines the integrity of her work, especially in the middle journals and the fiction.

Journal-keeping all those years may well have discouraged the full development of Nin's writing ability, as well as encouraged a satisfaction with first impressions rather than carefully crafted and reworked forms. Editing for Nin, according to her account, consisted "mostly of cutting"; the "act of rewriting" meant for her "tampering with the freshness and aliveness." Yet Nin cuts so much of the human and social context from her writing that at times it barely breathes at all. At the core of the problem is Nin's deep ambivalence about the autobiographical form. She was compelled to write from her own experience, had difficulty imagining other characters and worlds, yet she had a horror of revelations, of exposure to derision and abuse, as she imagined the consequences of such exposure to be. She hoped she would be "safe behind paper and ink and words," but the protective cloak of her writing proved all too transparent.

Nin's fiction is best appreciated in tandem with her Diary, since it is a variation on the autobiographical themes first set out in the journal. *House of Incest* is least in need of the Diary for support; it easily stands on its own as a fascinating surrealist descent into a woman's inner hell. The same is true for a handful of the stories in *Under a Glass Bell*, such as "The Labyrinth," "Birth," and "Hejda," which although derived from the Diary, have a highly wrought intensity and poetic condensation which are most effective. The first section of "Stella" is also extraordinarily compact and emotionally charged, but this novella does not fulfill the promise of the opening movement. The remainder of Nin's fiction subsequent to this point also disappoints as a whole. *Cities of the Interior* is an interesting experiment, but not a great work of art. Although it contains passages of subtlety and emotional power, overall the stylistic and structural problems detract significantly from the effectiveness of the work. Having removed the recognizable signposts from the outer world, clearly differentiated characters or fully elaborated metaphors or themes, Nin fails to substitute a stylistic perfection which might compensate for the unsubstantiality of her text. As a stylist, Nin is undeniably flawed, but as the author of a complex, enigmatic self-portrait of great richness and charm, Nin will continue to captivate readers of the future.

Notes and References

Preface

1. Maxwell Geismar, "Anaïs Nin: an Imprecise Spy in the House of Love," *Los Angeles Times,* 13 May 1979, 5:3.
2. Katha Politt, "Apologia Ended," *New York Times Book Review,* 13 July 1980, p. 7. The original diaries are in Special Collections, U.C.L.A. Library, inaccessible to the public. In addition to seven Diaries published so far, as well as two early Diaries posthumously published, two more early journals are to be published.
3. Marta Traba, "The Monumental 'I' of Anaïs Nin," *Under the Sign of Pisces* 7 (Winter 1976):14; Sharon Spencer, *Collage of Dreams* (Chicago, 1977), pp. 149–50; Mary Jane Moffat and Charlotte Painter, eds., *Revelations: Diaries of Women* (New York: Vintage Books, 1974), p. 86.
4. Term used by Richard Centing, review of Sharon Spencer's *Collage of Dreams, American Literature* 50 (November 1978):516.
5. Joyce Carol Oates, review of *The Diary of Anaïs Nin: 1955–1966, New York Times Book Review,* 27 June 1976, p. 4.
6. See Elaine Showalter, *A Literature of Their Own: British Women Novelists from Brontë to Lessing* (Princeton: Princeton University Press, 1977), Chap. 1; Sandra Gilbert and Susan Gubar, *The Madwoman in the Attic: The Woman Writer and the Nineteenth-Century Literary Imagination* (New Haven: Yale University Press, 1979), Part One.

Chapter One

1. The following abbreviations will be used in this book: *The Diary of Anaïs Nin: 1931–1934*—I; *1934–1939*—II; *1939–1944*—III; *1944–1947*—IV; *1947–1955*—V; *1955–1966*—VI; *1966–1974*—VII; *Linotte. The Early Diary of Anaïs Nin: 1914–1920*—L; *The Early Diary of Anaïs Nin: 1920–1923*—E; *The Novel of the Future*—NF. Please note that the published Diary is capitalized in this study and the unpublished diary is in lower case.
2. See John M. Bennett's review of a Joaquín Nin publication, *Pro Arte E Ideas Y Comentarios,* in *Under the Sign of Pisces* 6 (Winter 1975):6–9.
3. Marie Bashkirtseff, *The Journal of a Young Artist 1860–1884,* trans. Mary J. Serrano (New York: Cassell & Co., 1889), p. 178.
4. Harry T. Moore, Introduction to *D. H. Lawrence: An Unprofessional Study* (Chicago, 1964), p. 10.

135

5. Edmund Wilson, review of "This Hunger," in IV, 85.

6. Henry Miller, "Un Etre Etoilique," reprinted in *The Cosmological Eye* (New York, 1939), p. 269.

7. See Jay Martin, *Always Merry and Bright: The Life of Henry Miller* (Santa Barbara, 1978), Chap. 14.

8. In addition to "Un Etre Etoilique," Miller wrote another piece, "More About Anaïs Nin," in *Sunday after the War* (Norfolk, Conn.: New Directions, 1944), pp. 276–97.

9. Sharon Spencer asserts that Proust's influence on Nin has been the "most profound," in *Collage of Dreams*, Chap. 7.

10. Nin shared with the symbolists a preference for indirect statement, a position of detachment from society, cultivation of private sentiments. See Edmund Wilson, *Axel's Castle: A Study in the Imaginative Literature of 1870–1930* (New York: Charles Scribner's Sons, 1931).

11. "Waste of Timelessness," in *Waste of Timelessness and Other Early Stories* (Weston, Conn., 1977), pp. 1–6.

Chapter Two

1. George Gusdorf, "Conditions and Limits of Autobiography," in *Autobiography: Essays Theoretical and Critical,* ed. James Olney (Princeton: Princeton University Press, 1980), p. 43.

2. The seven volumes of the Diary edited by Nin with the assistance of Gunther Stuhlmann are distinguished in this study from the two early Diaries, presumably unedited, published after Nin's death. Although the seventh volume was also posthumously published, Nin apparently had completed the essential editing of this volume.

3. Quoted in Gusdorf, "Conditions," p. 44.

4. The following abbreviations of the fiction (appearing in parentheses in the text) will be used in this study: *Winter of Artifice*–WA; Under a Glass Bell—UGB; Ladders to Fire—LF; Children of the Albatross—CA; The Four-Chambered Heart—FH; A Spy in the House of Love—SPH; Seduction of the Minotaur—SM.

5. Walt Whitman, *Leaves of Grass,* ed. Harold W. Blodgett and Sculley Bradley (New York: New York University Press, 1965), p. 88.

6. Spencer uses the term in *Collage of Dreams*, Chap. 1.

7. This is suggested by Duane Schneider in "Anaïs Nin in the *Diary:* The Creation and Development of a Persona," *Mosaic* (Winter 1978):10–11.

8. Roy Pascal, *Design and Truth in Autobiography* (Cambridge: Harvard University Press, 1960), p. 184.

9. Carolyn Heilbrun and Catharine Stimpson, "Theories of Feminist Criticism: A Dialogue," in *Feminist Literary Criticism,* ed. Josephine Donovan (Lexington: University Press of Kentucky, 1975), p. 62.

10. Cited by Estelle C. Jelinek, "Anaïs Nin: A Critical Evaluation," in *Feminist Criticism: Essays on Theory, Poetry and Prose,* ed. Cheryl L. Brown and Karen Olson (Metuchen, N.J.: Scarecrow Press, 1978), p. 316.

11. The term is used by Lynn Z. Bloom and Orlee Holder in "Anaïs Nin's *Diary* in Context," in *Women's Autobiography: Essays in Criticism,* ed. Estelle C. Jelinek (Bloomington, 1980), p. 213.

12. Ibid., pp. 207–8.

13. Virginia Woolf, *The Diary of Virginia Woolf: Volume One, 1915–1919,* ed. Anne Olivier Bell (New York: Harcourt Brace Jovanovich, 1977), p. 266.

14. Lionel Trilling, *Sincerity and Authenticity* (Cambridge: Harvard University Press, 1972), pp. 10–11.

15. Oliver Evans, *Anaïs Nin* (Carbondale, 1968), p. 4.

16. Bettina Knapp, *Anaïs Nin,* (New York, 1978) Chap. 1.

17. Bruce Mazlish, "Autobiography and Psycho-analysis: Between Truth and Self-Deception," *Encounter* 35 (1970):37.

18. Elinor Langer, "Confessing," *Ms* 3 (December 1974):71.

19. Gilbert and Gubar, *Madwoman,* p. 49.

20. See Una Stannard, "The Mask of Beauty," in *Woman in Sexist Society,* ed. Vivian Gornick and Barbara K. Moran (New York: New American Library, 1971), pp. 187–203.

21. Both are quoted in Trilling, *Sincerity,* p. 119.

22. The word "persona" comes from the Latin meaning "actor's mask," and was adapted by the psychologist Carl Jung to mean the social mask we wear to meet the world, composed of society's expectations of who we should be. This mask offers a certain protection from exposure, while concealing those aspects of the individual (shadow) which may deviate significantly from this social facade. As a literary term, "persona" means the voice or voices projected by a writer in his/her work which are distinct from the writer's actual voice. Nin's Diary reveals both her literary and Jungian personae.

23. Colette, *The Vagabond,* trans. Enid McLeod (New York: Farrar, Straus & Giroux, 1955), p. 7.

24. Virginia Woolf, "Professions for Women," in *The Death of the Moth and Other Essays* (New York: Harcourt Brace Jovanovich, 1942), p. 237.

25. Kenneth Burke, *The Philosophy of Literary Form: Studies in Symbolic Action,* rev. ed. (New York: Vintage Books, 1957), p. 78.

26. Ironically, *Delta of Venus* was on the best-seller list in Europe and America, unlike the rest of Nin's work. While the writing in *Delta* is very effective as erotica, in the limited space available here, I do not think a close study of it is warranted.

Chapter Three

1. Quoted in Pascal, *Design and Truth,* p. 47.
2. From Anne Hollander, *Seeing through Clothes* (New York: Avon Press, 1980), Chap. 6.
3. Diane Wakoski, "A Tribute to Anaïs Nin," in *A Casebook on Anaïs Nin,* ed. Robert Zaller (New York, 1974), p. 152.
4. Steven Shapiro, "The Dark Continent of Literature: Autobiography," *Comparative Literature Studies* 5 (1968):434. Shapiro also remarks that the mirror-window motif is one of the "dominant themes in autobiography."
5. Margaret Atwood, *Surfacing* (New York: Popular Library, 1976), p. 205.
6. The phrase is Simone de Beauvoir's in *The Second Sex,* trans. H. M. Parshley (New York: Bantam Books., 1961), p. 599 (subsequent page references in text). My use of the term "narcissism" is based on my assumption that Nin's persona in the Diary fits the standard psychoanalytic definition of the narcissistic personality: "A) grandiose sense of self-importance or uniqueness, B) preoccupation with fantasies of unlimited success, power, brilliance, beauty, or ideal love, C) exhibitionism (the person requires constant attention and admiration), D) . . . marked feelings of rage, inferiority, shame, humiliation, or emptiness in response to criticism, indifference of others, or defeat. . . ." From Salman Akhtar and J. Anderson Thomson, Jr. "Overview: Narcissistic Personality Disorder," *American Journal of Psychiatry* 139 (January 1982):17.
7. Gilbert and Gubar and Showalter see images of confinement as one of the primary motifs of nineteenth-century women writers.
8. The "enclosed and secret room" has been a favorite symbol of women writers since Brontë's *Jane Eyre.* See Showalter, *Literature of Their Own,* p. 33.
9. Martin, *Always Merry,* p. 247.
10. Henry Miller, *Henry Miller Letters to Anaïs Nin,* (New York, 1965), p. 86.
11. Ibid., p. 33.
12. *Always Merry,* p. 308–9.
13. Wallace Stevens, *The Necessary Angel: Essays on Reality and the Imagination* (New York: Vintage Books, 1951), p. 6.
14. Katherine Mansfield, *Journal of Katherine Mansfield,* ed. J. Middleton Murry (New York: Alfred A. Knopf, 1959), pp. 5–6.
15. Virginia Woolf, *The Diary of Virginia Woolf: Volume Three, 1925–1930* (New York, 1980), p. 62.
16. See Nin's response to my dissertation on her work as an example (VII, 289–90, under the name Zee).
17. René Girard, "Narcissism: The Freudian Myth Demythified by Proust," in *Psychoanalysis, Creativity, and Literature: A French-American Inquiry,* ed. Alan Roland (New York: Columbia University Press, 1978), p. 293.
18. Christopher Lasch, *The Culture of Narcissism: American Life in an Age of Diminishing Expectations* (New York: W. W. Norton & Co., 1978), p. 91.

Chapter Four

1. *House of Incest* (Chicago: Swallow Press, 1958). Page references in text.
2. Cited in Evans, *Anaïs Nin,* p. 26.
3. Gilbert and Gubar, *Madwoman,* pp. 15–16.
4. Enid Rhodes Peschel, trans., introduction to Arthur Rimbaud, *A Season in Hell, The Illuminations* (New York: Oxford University Press, 1973), p. 7.
5. J. H. Matthews, *Surrealism and the Novel* (Ann Arbor: University of Michigan Press, 1966), p. 33.
6. See Philip K. Jason, "Doubles/Don Juans: Anaïs Nin and Otto Rank," *Mosaic* 11 (Winter 1978):81–94.
7. Martin, *Always Merry,* p. 43.
8. Nin's choice of Atlantis seems prophetic in light of current views of Atlantis as the "lost continent of the female tradition." See Showalter, *Literature of Their Own,* p. 10, Gubar and Gilbert, *Madwoman,* p. 102.
9. See my essay, "Anaïs Nin's *House of Incest* and Ingmar Bergman's *Persona:* Two Variations on a Theme," *Literature/Film Quarterly* 7, no. 1 (1979):47–59.
10. Sylvia Plath, *Ariel* (New York: Harper & Row, 1966), p. 9.
11. This parallel is developed in John Tytell's "Anaïs Nin and 'The Fall of the House of Usher,'" *Pisces* 2 (Winter 1971):5–11.
12. Cited in Anna Balakian, *Surrealism: The Road to the Absolute* (New York: Dutton, 1970), p. 243.

Chapter Five

1. *Winter of Artifice,* first published in 1939 by Obelisk Press, included "Djuna," "Lilith," and "The Voice." "Djuna," the Nin-Henry-June story, was never reprinted; "Lilith," in revised form became "Winter," and "The Voice" was revised under the same name. Nin's Gemor Press edition came out in 1942, and in 1961 Swallow Press published *Winter,* including "Stella," originally published in 1942 as "This Hunger." Page references are to the Swallow edition.
2. Benjamin Franklin V and Duane Schneider point this out in their book *Anaïs Nin: An Introduction* (Athens, 1979), p. 27.
3. *The Winter of Artifice,* Villa Seurat Series (Paris; Obelisk Press, 1939), p. 176.
4. Ibid, p. 178.
5. Evans, *Anaïs Nin,* p. 46.

Chapter Six

1. Cited in Evans, *Anaïs Nin,* p. 64.
2. Ibid.
3. Edmund Wilson, "Books—Doubts and Dreams: *Dangling Man* and *Under a Glass Bell,*" *The New Yorker* 20 (1 April 1944):73.
4. Elizabeth Hardwick, "Fiction Chronicle," *Partisan Review* 15 (June 1948):705.

5. Ibid., p. 707.

6. *Under a Glass Bell* (New York: Gemor Press, 1944). Page references in text.

7. Franklin and Schneider go further in their book, stating "a glass bell covers not only this story and its characters, but all the stories in the volume and virtually all of Nin's fiction," p. 50.

Chapter Seven

1. *Ladders to Fire* was originally published in 1946 in different form, *Children of the Albatross* in 1947, *The Four-Chambered Heart* in 1950, *A Spy in the House of Love* in 1954, *Solar Barque* in 1958, later incorporated into *Seduction of the Minotaur* in 1961. For more detail on changes in text, see Franklin and Schneider's *Anaïs Nin* and Franklin's *Anaïs Nin: A Bibliography* (Kent, 1973).

2. Abbreviations used in this chapter include, in order of publication, *Ladders, Children, Heart, Spy,* and *Seduction.*

3. Sharon Spencer, Introduction to *Cities of the Interior* (Chicago: Swallow Press, 1974), p. xi.

4. Knapp, *Anaïs Nin,* p. 96.

5. Frank Baldanza, "Anaïs Nin," *Minnesota Review* 2 (Winter 1962):263–71.

6. The entire prologue is quoted in Franklin and Schneider, *Anaïs Nin,* p. 64.

7. Cf. Suzette A. Henke, "Anaïs Nin: Bread and Wafer," *Pisces* 7 (Spring 1976):7–17.

Chapter Eight

1. Spencer, *Collage,* p. 115.

2. Evans, *Anaïs Nin,* p. 181.

Selected Bibliography

PRIMARY SOURCES

1. Diaries

The Diary of Anaïs Nin: 1931–1934. New York: Harcourt, Brace & World, 1966.
The Diary of Anaïs Nin: 1934–1939. New York: Harcourt, Brace & World, 1967.
The Diary of Anaïs Nin: 1939–1944. New York: Harcourt, Brace & World, 1969.
The Diary of Anaïs Nin: 1944–1947. New York: Harcourt Brace Jovanovich, 1971.
The Diary of Anaïs Nin: 1947–1955. New York: Harcourt Brace Jovanovich, 1974.
The Diary of Anaïs Nin: 1955–1966. New York: Harcourt Brace Jovanovich, 1976.
The Diary of Anaïs Nin: 1966–1974. New York: Harcourt Brace Jovanovich, 1980.
The Early Diary of Anaïs Nin: 1920–1923. New York: Harcourt Brace Jovanovich, 1982.
Linotte. The Early Diary of Anaïs Nin: 1914–1920. New York: Harcourt Brace Jovanovich, 1978.

2. Fiction

Children of the Albatross. New York: E. P. Dutton, 1947.
Cities of the Interior. New York: Edwards Brother, 1959.
Collages. Denver: Alan Swallow, 1964.
Delta of Venus: Erotica. New York: Harcourt Brace Jovanovich, 1977.
The Four-Chambered Heart. New York: Duell, Sloan & Pearce, 1950.
The House of Incest. Paris: Siana Editions, 1936.
Ladders to Fire. New York: E. P. Dutton, 1946.
Little Birds: Erotica. New York: Harcourt Brace Jovanovich, 1979.
Solar Barque. New York: Edwards Brothers, 1958. Expanded as *Seduction of the Minotaur*. Denver: Alan Swallow, 1961.
A Spy in the House of Love. New York: British Book Centre, 1954.
This Hunger. New York: Gemor Press, 1945.
Under a Glass Bell. New York: Gemor Press, 1944.

Waste of Timelessness and Other Early Stories. Weston, Conn.: Magic Circle Press, 1977.
The Winter of Artifice. Paris: Obelisk Press, 1939.

3. Selected Nonfiction
D. H. Lawrence: An Unprofessional Study. Paris: Edward W. Titus, 1932.
In Favor of the Sensitive Man, and Other Essays. New York: Harcourt Brace Jovanovich, 1976.
The Novel of the Future. New York: Macmillan Co., 1968.
"On Writing." Hanover, N.H.: Daniel Oliver Associates, 1947.
"Realism and Reality." New York: Alicat Book Shop, 1946.
A Woman Speaks: The Lectures, Seminars and Interviews of Anaïs Nin. Edited by Evelyn J. Hinz. Chicago: Swallow Press, 1975.

SECONDARY SOURCES

1. Bibliographies
Cutting, Rose Marie. *Anaïs Nin: A Reference Guide.* Boston: G. K. Hall, 1978. Useful annotated bibliography.
Franklin, Benjamin V. *Anaïs Nin: A Bibliography.* Kent, Ohio: Kent State University Press, 1973.

2. Books and Essay Collections
Centing, Richard, ed. *Under the Sign of Pisces: Anaïs Nin and Her Circle* 1–12 (1970–1981). Quarterly devoted to Nin for eleven years; contains some valuable essays. Now published by Centing as *Sea Horse.*
Evans, Oliver. *Anaïs Nin.* Carbondale: Southern Illinois University Press, 1968. First book-length study of Nin's work; discussion of fiction still useful.
Franklin, Benjamin V., and Schneider, Duane. *Anaïs Nin.* Athens: Ohio University Press, 1979. First good study of the Diary; better balanced than its predecessors.
Hinz, Evelyn J. *The Mirror and the Garden: Realism and Reality in the Writings of Anaïs Nin.* Columbus: Ohio State University Libraries, 1971. Early defense of Nin's writing.
————, ed. *Mosaic* 11 (Winter 1978). "The World of Anaïs Nin." Best collection of essays on Nin's writing.
Knapp, Bettina. *Anaïs Nin.* New York: Frederick Ungar Publishing Co., 1978. Appreciative study of Nin.
Martin, Jay. *Always Merry and Bright: The Life of Henry Miller.* Santa Barbara: Capra Press, 1978. Fundamental biographical source.

Miller, Henry. *Letters to Anaïs Nin.* Edited by Gunther Stuhlmann. New York: G. P. Putnam's Sons, 1965.
Spencer, Sharon. *Collage of Dreams: The Writings of Anaïs Nin.* Chicago: Swallow Press, 1977. Imaginative study; more appreciative than critical.
Zaller, Robert, ed. *A Casebook on Anaïs Nin.* New York: New American Library, 1974. Contains many valuable early essays.

3. Selected Articles

Baldanza, Frank. "Anaïs Nin." *Minnesota Review* 2 (Winter 1962):263–71. Critical discussion of stylistic failure in Nin's early writing.
Bloom Lynn Z., and Holder, Orlee. "Anaïs Nin's *Diary* in Context," in *Women's Autobiography: Essays in Criticism,* edited by Estelle C. Jelinek. Bloomington: Indiana University Press, 1980, pp. 206–20. Place Nin's Diary in female autobiographical tradition.
Killoh, Ellen Peck. "The Woman Writer and the Element of Destruction." *College English* 34 (October 1972):31–38. Discusses Nin's effort to turn herself into ideal woman artist.
Mazzocco, Robert. "To Tell You the Truth." *New York Review of Books,* 8 September 1966, pp. 6, 8. Good critique of the Diary's "truthfulness."
Miller, Henry. "Un Etre Etoilique." *Criterion* 17 (October 1937):33–52. One of the best essays on Nin's work.
Oates, Joyce Carol. "A Gigantic Plea for Understanding." Review of *The Diary of Anaïs Nin 1955–1966* and *In Favor of the Sensitive Man and Other Essays. New York Times Book Review,* 27 June 1976, pp. 4, 5. Sympathetic, insightful commentary on the Diary.
Pollitt, Katha. "Apologia Ended." Review of *The Diary of Anaïs Nin 1966–1974. New York Times Book Review,* 13 July 1980, pp. 7, 24. Sharp critique of the Diary's limitations.
Sukenick, Lynn. "The Diaries of Anaïs Nin." *Shenandoah* 27 (Spring 1976):96–103. Elegantly written defense of Nin's writing.
Traba, Marta. "The Monumental 'I' of Anaïs Nin." *Under the Sign of Pisces* 7 (Winter 1976):8–14. Demystification of Nin's Diary.
Wolcott, James. "Life Among the Ninnies." Review of *The Diary of Anaïs Nin: 1966–1974. New York Review of Books,* 26 June 1980, p. 21. Nin's career as a masterpiece of self-promotion.

Index

DATE DUE			

DEMCO 38-297